AN
ANTI-CORRUPTION
MANUAL
FOR
ADMINISTRATORS
IN
LAW ENFORCEMENT

AN ANTI-CORRUPTION MANUAL FOR ADMINISTRATORS IN LAW ENFORCEMENT

by
Richard H. Ward
University of Illinois
and
Robert McCormack
John Jay College of Criminal Justice

THE JOHN JAY PRESS
New York
1979

First Edition, 1979
Copyright © 1979 The John Jay Press

Prepared under Grant Number 75NI-99-0083 from the National Institute of Law Enforcement and Criminal Justice, Law Enforcement Assistance Administration, U.S. Department of Justice.

Points of view or opinions in this document are those of the authors and do not necessarily represent the official position or politics of the U.S. Department of Justice.

Manufactured in the United States of America

ISBN: 0-89444-008-X

Table of Contents

Acknowledgments

As authors of this manual, we wish to thank the many members of the law enforcement community who helped in the preparation of this work. We are particularly grateful to those who responded to the national internal affairs survey, to those who agreed to interviews with Project staff members conducting field surveys throughout the country, and to those active participants who conducted and attended Project workshops.

We would also like to thank the members of the Law Enforcement Assistance Administration, particularly David Farmer and Phillip Travers, for their advice and assistance and Harry O'Reilly, Terrance D. McCann, and Dennis N. Butler of the New York City Police for their work in reviewing and suggesting revisions in our original manuscript and for developing much of the material in Chapter 8.

Much of the basic work on this manual could not have been done without Antony E. Simpson's review of the literature of police corruption and without Nina Duchaine's annotated bibliography of that literature. We are indebited to them as well as to the authors of the ten monographs developed by the Project: Charles Bahn, Herbert Biegel, Dorothy Bracey, David Burnham, Janet E. Fishman, William McCarthy, Alan Shealy, Lawrence Sherman, and Mitchell Ware.

We would also like to extend our appreciation to the members of the Advisory Board of the Anti-Corruption Management Project for their guidance during the twenty-two month period of the L.E.A.A. grant. The national reputation and experience of Board members like Attorney Thomas Decker, Commissioner Robert di Grazia, Chief James Parsons, Professors Lorn Phelps and Albert Reiss provided the Project staff with entree into a number of law enforcement agencies. They also helped in the selection and organization of material for this book, and to them and to all of the other people we have mentioned, we can only express our hope that this manual justifies the support and help we have received.

— Richard H. Ward
University of Illinois
— Robert McCormack
John Jay College of Criminal Justice

AN
ANTI-CORRUPTION
MANUAL
FOR
ADMINISTRATORS
IN
LAW ENFORCEMENT

Introduction

Corruption is not a problem limited to the police; it is a national phenomenon which affects private lives and virtually every level of government. Nevertheless, police corruption and other kinds of misconduct are of serious concern to the police administrator who must recognize them as potentially threatening to the effectiveness of the organization. The very nature of the police function subjects officers to tempting offers, and public confidence, which is necessary for a police department to function effectively, must be built on the knowledge that a department protects the rights of citizens impartially and professionally. To implement any successful anti-corruption program, a police administrator must have the whole-hearted support and cooperation of authorities who make political appointments. He must be allowed to address problems in a climate that is free of political involvement. However, the mayor of a city and other high ranking officials must be kept aware of all current and anticipated changes to be made. Changes like demotions, promotions, or firings will often require the approval of the mayor. Involve-

ment of the mayor and other appropriate officials with the
first changes to be made will insure the administrator's control and successful implementation of an anti-corruption
program. Regular reporting sessions, preferably weekly,
should be scheduled to keep political authorities informed of
the program and to avoid premature, embarrassing stories in
the media.

Corruption takes many forms, ranging from the acceptance
of a small gift to the acceptance of large sums of money or
other considerations for overlooking illegal activity. Corruption is insidious, for it weakens the framework of an organization, and once discovered and exposed, it may result in a
backlash of public sentiment that may take years to overcome. Because the police are viewed as the vanguard of law
enforcement, discovery of corrupt activities within a police
department is more likely to have a detrimental effect than
the revelation of corruption in other areas of government.
The indictment or conviction of a judge or a lawyer does not
generally bring discredit upon all lawyers, but unfortunately the arrest of a police officer frequently discredits his or
her whole department.

Many definitions of corruption exist, and what may be acceptable in one community may not be in another. Usually,
however, the level of integrity in a police department may
reflect the culture and mores of the society it polices. Despite
differences in local attitudes, most police officers know when
they are doing something wrong. They are aware of those
activities for which they will be punished or dismissed. There
are, however, some vaguely defined areas of police misconduct. The acceptance of free coffee is not viewed as misconduct by most police officers (Fishman, 1978). The Project
staff found that the acceptance of a free meal brought more
mixed reactions from police, and the acceptance of a gift,
probably a common practice in many departments, is viewed
by most officers as a form of misconduct. The acceptance of
money for overlooking a traffic violation or a criminal act is
viewed as corrupt by almost all police officers. Nevertheless
many officers continue their involvement in activities which
are corrupt.

Analyses indicate that the level of misconduct or corruption is generally related to the quality and style of manage-

ment in a department and to the chief's commitment to eliminating such conduct. Public attitudes toward acceptance by police of small gratuities may often be determined by the size of the department, salaries of police, and public perception of police effectiveness.

Although some totally dedicated chief administrators have attempted to eliminate corruption with little success, the reasons for their failure vary; some failures involved external variables beyond the chief's control. However, those failures can also be attributed in some measure to the management, policies, and procedures practiced within the department.

This manual is designed to assist a new or incumbent chief administrator to create a healthy climate of integrity within his department. The chief's attitude is crucial; if he is not sincere, little can be accomplished. Furthermore, the administrator and his management staff must be willing to accept the fact that corruption may exist, must be willing to move against all of those involved in it, and must be able to accept criticism of a strong, anti-corruption policy. Most police departments are insular, and frequently for what appears to be good reason, departmental members will cover up or downplay corrupt acts and misconduct. The chief who fails to act against corruption is watching the burning fuse of a bomb which, especially when media and political overview are great, could explode at any time.

The facts of political life cannot be ignored, especially in a discussion of corruption, and a chief must recognize the importance of developing a political climate in which an active anti-corruption campaign will not collapse and result in the chief's removal. Forces in political life and in organized crime support corruption, and they are frequently powerful enough to destroy an anti-corruption campaign.

The authors have attempted to develop a practical book which provides management aids and techniques to fight corruption and realistic information to resolve the political and organizational problems that may occur due to an anti-corruption campaign.

The authors also initiated with the cooperation of the Advisory Board of the Anti-Corruption Management Project two intensive reviews of the historical and contemporary literature of police corruption (Simpson, 1977; Duchaine,

1979). These surveys included unpublished and published works, including material from European, Asian, and African countries.

The materials in this manual are based upon hundreds of interviews, the results of questionnaire surveys, a historical analysis of corruption, and information garnered from four workshops on police corruption during a period of twenty months. On-site visits were made to more than a dozen police departments, and interviews were conducted with police chiefs, unit heads, and members of internal affairs units. The authors, who have thirty years of police experience, have visited almost every major American police department during the last five years. The Advisory Board to the Anti-Corruption Management Project also provided a wealth of experience and practical information, much of which has been incorporated in this manual. Although the primary emphasis is to provide a manual which will be of practical value to the police administrator, it is hoped that this book will be helpful to other administrators confronted with corruption in government, politics, business, and other areas of the criminal justice system.

Defining, Locating, and Measuring Corruption

I
Determining the Level of Corrupt Activity

One of the major problems facing police administrators is determining whether or not corruption exists, and if it does, in what areas and to what extent does it occur.

In defining what constitutes corruption for a police department, a chief has a certain amount of administrative latitude to establish policy within legal limits. His administrative discretion should certainly be tempered by professional police ethics. In the process of formulating a definition of corruption, a chief must not "over-corruptionalize" in the way that legislatures have "over-criminalized" certain behavior. Good anti-corruption policy is well defined, practical, enforceable, workable, and realistic. Different communities have different standards of what is sociable and what is corrupt, and a chief should realistically consider community norms when defining corruption and formulating policy.

Locating corruption depends upon how corruption is

defined. In light of a definition, particular situations and circumstances can be assessed as potentially corrupt. Tradition-
ally corrupt situations in law enforcement involve laws concerning commercialized vice. In situations of "victimless"
crimes, police officers are tempted to rationalize corrupt
practices, particularly when the seriousness of a charge will
determine lenient court treatment later. Undoubtedly, this
area of enforcement will be the most troublesome for administrators.

Several approaches can be used to determine the existence of corruption. Some police administrators, however,
do not act aggressively against potential corruption or misconduct by police. Accustomed to reacting to daily crises,
they assume that their department is not prone to corruption. They depend upon reports from other municipal
agencies, rumors and gossip, and complaints from citizens
to call their attention to corrupt behavior. They are caught
by surprise when they learn from a newspaper article or
a television report that their employees are engaging in
corrupt practices. For these administrators, a periodic review of the corrupt activities and practices listed in Tables
1 and 2 is suggested as insurance against unpreparedness
and potential corruption.

Most administrators depend upon the efforts of their internal affairs or inspections units to identify areas of corruption or misconduct. However, during the last decade
these units were operating in almost every department
where corruption was discovered and were usually staffed
by honest, capable individuals. Why, then, did they fail to
uncover corruption before it was exposed by some external
force?

THE VARIETY OF CORRUPTION

While conducting the research necessary for this manual,
staff members of the Project visited numerous police departments. In one Mid-western department, noted for its integrity, the commander of the internal affairs division stated

that no corruption or misconduct existed in the department and that any illegal acts involving two or more officers could not occur for any length of time because of departmental procedures established to identify offenders. A week later, four officers of the department were arrested for operating a burglary ring. Although the burglary ring was probably an isolated instance of corruption, visits to many police departments revealed that frequently the internal affairs units were unaware of what police were doing in the streets. Furthermore, although most internal affairs units respond to complaints, they do not generally initiate investigations.

Another issue which must be confronted is that of definition of terms. The staff of the Project found that certain types of conduct or misconduct, tolerated and accepted in some departments, are considered corrupt by other departments. In one department, the chief stated that corruption was not a problem, but after further questioning, he admitted that there was a problem of "misconduct." It was observed that many of the acts for which his officers were being investigated would have been considered corrupt in other departments. Some departments perceived taking a free cup of coffee as a corrupt act, whereas most departments did not view the acceptance of free coffee as a problem. The staff did not find one department in which accepting a cup of coffee was considered unusual. No doubt, there are some, but they appear to be in the minority.

DEFINITIONS

No single definition of corruption appears to be satisfactory, and surveys indicate a wide range of opinion and policies about it. Perhaps the most satisfactory definition, devised from the results of questionnaires sent to some five hundred police departments is the following:

> Police corruption consists of acts which involve the misuse of police authority for the police employee's personal gain: activity of the police employee which compromises, or has the potential to compromise, his ability to enforce the law or provide other service im-

partially; the protection of illicit activities from police enforcement, whether or not the police employee's involvement in promoting the business of one person while discouraging that of another person. (National Advisory Commission, 1973, p. 473.)

Although this definition does apply to the acceptance of a free cup of coffee, it also applies to the pervasive forms of activity which are detrimental to the operations and image of a department. Corrupt activities range from a free meal or small gratuity to serious, obvious acts like accepting bribes to overlook violations, which are widely accepted as being corrupt. Corruption, as it is defined in this manual, focuses on illegal acts which result in personal gain. Physical abuse as a form of corruption is excluded, because as Herman Goldstein noted:

Corruption and physical abuse are sometimes inseparable. Police have, for example, been known to use force or the threat of force to obtain payoffs. But most of the complaints alleging improper use of force do not include charges of corruption for personal gain. (Goldstein, 1975, p. 3)

Apparently, no single definition of corruption will have universal application. However, the kinds of corruption discussed in this manual have a conspiratorial nature. Corrupt acts by an individual officer in a barely visable situation may go undetected, and the police administrator can only rely on an alert internal affairs unit to keep these acts to a minimum. To deal generally with the concept of corruption, it is necessary to provide definitions which are loosely constructed and often non-specific. As with the crime specific programs recently developed to deal with the uniqueness of individual crimes (Urban Institute, 1975; Ward, 1974), specific tactics must be developed to address the uniqueness of each corruption typology.

IDENTIFYING CORRUPT ACTS

Barker and Roebuck (1974) have identified eight forms of

corrupt activity, and Goldstein (1975) has identified eleven "schemes." Many of these activities can be classified in the so-called "grey areas" of police corruption; the activities seem to involve ill-defined and vague ethical choices. The experience of this Project has indicated that "grey areas" are "grey" simply because the policy of the administration is unclear or purposely vague. In large departments with serious corruption problems, the tolerance of minor improprieties like free meals or free admissions to entertainment is high. As one police official said, "The first job of a chief is to stay in office; therefore, he has to deal with things on a priority basis. Besides, cracking down on that kind of stuff is bad for morale."

Many of the activities identified by Barker, Roebuck, and Goldstein are generally accepted as being corrupt by police administrators. These activities can generally be classified into four categories:

1. Acts which are common throughout the whole department and are generally accepted.
2. Acts which are less common than those of the first category but which are generally overlooked.
3. Acts which are common to particular units, like narcotics and vice, and which are accepted or overlooked by unit members.
4. Acts which are not common, which involve a few individuals, and which would be reported if discovered.

Activities included in the first three categories are generally identifiable. Activities in the fourth category usually involve relatively few individuals, and discovery is difficult. Generally, the administrator will be aware of activities in the first category, but probably he will be unaware of activities in the second and third categories. Acts in the second and third categories usually create a major corruption problem if they are not identified and eliminated. Investigation of these acts is difficult, because they are performed by a minority of members in a department and because they are usually overlooked or accepted. Frequently, an internal affairs unit is aware of such acts but does not investigate them unless a specific complaint is made.

The administrator interested in ascertaining the levels of misconduct or corruption has several options available to him. He can depend on his internal affairs unit; he can assign

TABLE 1

TYPE	ACT AND ACTORS	THOSE WHO CORRUPT	SUPPORT FROM PEER GROUP	ORGANIZATION CONTENT	POLICE DEPARTMENT'S REACTION
1. Corruption of authority	Free meals, liquor, services, discounts, free admissions to entertainment and rewards	Respectable citizens	Many groups consider this nondeviant behavior when coming from high status	No organization	Acceptance or mild disapproval
2. Kickbacks	Money, goods, and services from towing companies, ambulances, garages, lawyers, doctors, bondsmen, undertakers, taxicabs, service stations, moving companies, etc.	Legitimate businesses	Viewed as "clean" fringe benefits	Collusion between businessmen and policemen	Acceptance and mild disapproval for goods and services, suspension or dismissal for cash kickbacks.
3. Opportunistic Theft: from suspects victims, crime scenes, and unprotected property	Thefts from suspects, crime scenes, and unprotected property	Corrupt officers and unsuspecting victims. Violation of criminal norms Larceny, grand and petty	Depends on: peer groups, informal policy of accepting or rejecting "clean" money, value of the theft and the secrecy of the theft	No organization—opportunistic	Mild disapproval, admonitions and warnings, suspensions, dismissals, and criminal proceedings.
4. Shakedowns	Money from criminal or traffic violators	Criminals or citizens Violation of criminal norms Extortion	Degree of support contingent on: informal policy concerning "clean" money, identity of those who corrupt and secrecy of the act.	No organization—opportunistic	Suspension or dismissal

TABLE 1 (Continued)

TYPE	ACT AND ACTORS	THOSE WHO CORRUPT	SUPPORT FROM PEER GROUP	ORGANIZATION CONTENT	POLICE DEPARTMENT'S REACTION
5. Protection of illegal activities	Protection money from vice operators or legitimate companies operating illegally	Criminals and legitimate businessmen Violations of criminal norms Bribery	Hinges on policy of accepting or rejecting "clean" money, identity of the corruptor and the secrecy of the transaction	Exhibits bureaucratic structure	Departments may block investigations
6. The Fix	Quashing of prosecution Disposal of traffic tickets	Criminals and citizens Violation of criminal norms Bribery	Most peer groups oppose sale of criminal cases, although some may condone sale of misdemeanor cases and fixing traffic tickets	Fixers may be maintained on a payroll	Dismissal and/or criminal prosecution
7. Direct Criminal Activities	Burglaries, robberies	Police directly commit crimes against persons or property Violation of criminal norms Burglary and robbery	No support from peer group	Small working groups of corrupt officers	Dismissal and criminal prosecution
8. Internal Payoffs	Sale of work assignments, off-days, holidays, vacation periods, evidence and promotion	Exclusively police officers Violation of criminal norms Extortion and bribery	Most peer groups oppose this criminal activity	May be organized within departments engaged in illegal types of corruption	Varies from acceptance and protection to dismissal on criminal prosecution

SOURCE: Barker and Roebuck

TABLE 2
"VARIOUS SCHEMES"
COMMON CORRUPT PRACTICES

Listed below are some of the most common corrupt practices in which police have been known to engage in their dealings with citizens. The list is by no means exhaustive. It does, however, identify most of the major areas where a police agency is vulnerable.

1. Failing to arrest and prosecute those the officer knows have violated the law.

  Examples: Motorists parked overtime or illegally.

  Traffic violators including drunk drivers (the "traffic-fix" being perhaps the most common).

  Gamblers, prostitutes, narcotics users, homosexuals.

  Violators of minor regulatory ordinances, such as those regulating business hours.

  Violators of the conditions of a license administered by the police agency.

  Juvenile offenders.

  More serious offenders such as burglars and persons engaged in organized criminal activity.

2. Agreeing to drop an investigation prematurely by not pursuing leads which would produce evidence supporting a criminal charge.

3. Agreeing not to inspect locations or premises where violations are known to occur and where an officer's presence might curtail the illegal activity.

  Example: Taverns in which prostitution or gambling flourishes and probably contributes to the volume of business.

4. Refraining from making arrests on licensed premises where an arrest would result in license review that could lead to revocation.

5. Reducing the seriousness of a charge against an offender.

6. Agreeing to alter testimony at trial or to provide less than the full amount of evidence available.

TABLE 2 (continued)

7. Providing more police protection or presence than is required by standard operating procedures.

    Examples: More frequent and intensive checks of the security of private premises.

                More frequent presence in a store or other commercial establishment, such as a hotel, club, or restaurant where the officer's presence benefits the owner by keeping out "undesirables."

                Observation of parked cars while owners attend a social gathering or meeting in an area where cars are commonly stolen or damaged.

                Escorting businessmen making bank deposits.

8. Influencing departmental recommendations regarding the granting of licenses.

    Example: Recommending for or against continuance of a liquor or amusement license by either giving or suppressing derogatory information.

9. Arranging access to confidential departmental records or agreeing to alter such records.

10. Referring individuals caught in a new and stressful situation to persons who can assist them and who stand to profit from the referral.

    Examples: Making referrals to bondsmen or defense attorneys.

                Placing accident victims in contact with physicians or attorneys specializing in the filing of personal injury claims.

                Arranging for delivery of bodies to a funeral home.

                Selecting the ambulance or tow truck summoned to the scene of an accident or an illegally parked car.

11. Appropriating for personal use or disposal items of value acquired on the job.

    Examples: Jewelry and goods from the scene of a burglary.

                Narcotics confiscated from users or peddlers.

                Funds used in gambling.

                Valuables found at the scene of a fire.

                Private property of a drunk or a deceased person.

                Confiscated weapons.

someone else to conduct an independent investigation; he can personally conduct an investigation; he can seek independent assistance. When an administrator suspects widespread misconduct, the views of an independent, unbiased investigator can be valuable. New York City's Knapp Commission used the services of investigators on leave from federal agencies like the F.B.I. and I.R.S.. Former members of federal and state investigative agencies can also be employed in external investigations. External resources available to the administrator are discussed in Chapter 6; the focus in this chapter is on utilizing departmental resources to investigate and determine the extent of the corruption if it exists.

SIGNS OF CORRUPTION

William McCarthy, a former Deputy Commissioner with the New York City Police Department, maintains that certain indicators exist which help determine whether or not a department is corrupt. These include:

> . . .Crime statistics, arrest and summons data, court records and street conditions such as solicitation for prostitution, gambling activity and widespread illegal parking, to name a few. (McCarthy, 1976).

Other indicators include reviews of administrative records, trends in citizen complaints, and interviews with citizens in key occupations.

REVIEWS OF ADMINISTRATIVE RECORDS

Although a review of all records is impossible, some attempt should be made to examine various reports and records on a random basis. Court records, particularly in specific crime categories like drunken driving, narcotics-trafficking, gambling, and prostitution can be helpful. The investigator should attempt to ascertain whether or not any patterns of corruption in records emerge. Are cases dismissed more frequently when a particular lawyer is involved? Are certain types of cases dismissed more frequently than others? Are weak affidavits being prepared?

Activity reports may indicate specific areas to be watched. Unusual activity or inactivity in serving summons may be indicative of corrupt acts.

Spot checks of crime reports may indicate a pattern of manipulation of major crime statistics, because corrupt police can reduce the seriousness of complaints. Narcotics and vice complaints are particularly susceptible to police manipulation. Missing or deleted entries in arrest records may be evidence of the release of arrested persons in exchange for some unlawful consideration. Geographic areas from which complaints are made may indicate potential corruption. Meyer writes:

> Evidence from other studies suggests that some forms of police corruption are found in specific areas. Conditions characteristic of individual city neighborhoods may be responsible for generating and supporting some, but not other kinds of corruption. . .The Commissioners [Knapp Commission] observations suggest that certain socioeconomic, crime or area-usage patterns account for the variance in the spatial distribution of corruption. (Meyer, 1977, p. 16).

There are also indicators that will apprise the administration that anti-corruption efforts are succeeding. As ethical requirements in an agency are strengthened and the process of internalization occurs, peer group pressure becomes supportive of demands for higher ethical conduct. In response, the agency must be prepared to support officers who report their peers for corrupt activities. In many departments reporting fellow officers for corrupt activities is routine. One officer told Project researchers that if caught by a fellow officer in any corrupt situation, he would be surprised if he were not reported.

REVIEWS OF ARREST RECORDS

Another indicator that ethical standards have been strenghtened is a gradual increase in the arrests of citizens for bribery. Although arrest policies for bribery should be encouraged, an administrator should supplement them with an aggressive campaign to educate the public against bribe-giving. As Bracey (1976) sympathetically declares:

> Related to the problems of laws that people don't want to obey are the problems of laws that people can't obey. Included here are such legal mazes as building codes, liquor laws, gun permit regulations and parking violation rules, which are designed to regulate rather than forbid these activities involved. The laws, regulations and ordinances governing these areas are often the result of piecemeal legislation, designed to cope with a specific situation and then incorporated into a general rule. Aspects of these codes are often the result of pressure by special interest groups, groups usually smaller and more numerous than those associated with unpopular laws (a block association, for example, may demand special parking regulations on its streets, increasing the convenience of residents but also adding to the general state of confusion surrounding on-street parking.)
> Given the fact that many of these regulatory statutes are vague, anachronistic and internally contradictory — and that they tend to be administered by bureaucracies that are elaborate and inefficient — there results a situation which makes it impossible for the most earnestly law-abiding citizen to conduct his lawful business in a lawful manner.

In many communities, public mores determine the ethical levels of police personnel. In some departments, however, police ethics are not determined by community expectations but by the level of integrity the administration demands of its personnel. That level of integrity is higher than that of the general community. In all departments there is a perceived level of corruption at which an officer is subject to sanctions.

MEASURING CORRUPTION

One method used by this Project to measure corruption or misconduct was the use of questionnaires. Questionnaires were found to be reliable in determining the level of unethical behavior acceptable by department standards. There are some indications that the tolerance level of misconduct revealed by the questionnaires is a symptom of more serious corruption than misconduct. The Knapp Commission Report provided evidence that low-level misconduct or "grass-eating" type of corruption is directly responsible for the code of silence which nurtures serious, systematic corruption. The research of the Project substantiates the Knapp Commission's conclusion.

A questionnaire was developed by the Anti-Corruption Management Project to test the feasibility of measuring police corruption. It was developed to be administered to police officers at roll calls in various law enforcement agencies throughout the country. The questionnaire was field tested and periodically revised as a result of constructive criticism from law enforcement officials.

To identify departments of high, medium, and low levels of integrity, the Project's Advisory Board was asked by the authors of the questionnaire to recommend agencies which, from their own personal information and experience, reflected a spectrum of high, medium, and low levels of integrity. The recommended agencies were contacted, and from among them, the target cities in which agencies were located were selected. A survey of the local newspapers in each target city was conducted for the previous two years to substantiate or refute the opinions of the Advisory Board regarding the ethical standards of the agencies. In addition, a random sample of five hundred citizens in each city was sent a questionnaire intended to compare community standards with prevailing police standards. In each city, the subsequent administration of the questionaire at police roll calls supported and substantiated data acquired in the survey and citizen questionnaires. Consequently, the Project believed that its questionnaire had successfully discriminated between the different ethical levels of the agencies.

McCORMACK-FISHMAN IMPROBITY SCALES

At various stages of development, the Project's questionnaire was composed of twenty-eight to forty questions. Some questions were discarded after analysis showed them to be faulty; others were added at the suggestion of Advisory Board members and the field officers to whom the questionnaire was administered. The three major segments of the questionnaire were the McCormack-Fishman Improbity Scales, based on the theory of Guttman Scaling described by Fishman (1978). This theory maintains that if respondents are given a series of three or more activities related in some way to a variable under consideration (unethical behavior), some of the activities may prove to be "harder" indicators of the variable than others. If, after being tested among several groups, an order or scale of "hardness" among items emerges that has a coefficient of reproduceability of 90% or over (in 90 cases of a 100 cases, groups will arrange the activities in the same order), the order or scale constitutes a Guttman scale for that sample of respondents. As a result, they and others may be rated or scored in relation to that Guttman scale.

The Project's questionnaire listed eight improbus activities which the researchers felt would be generally understandable to police officers throughout the country. The activities were listed randomly in the questionnaire as follows:

1. diff.   easy   a. accepting a free cup of coffee from a restaurant owner in your area.

2. diff.   easy   b. accepting a free meal from a restaurant owner in your patrol area.

3. diff.   easy   c. accepting sums of money on a systematic basis to allow a gambler to operate.

4. diff.   easy   d. accepting gifts from a towing company for preferential treatment at accident scenes.

5. diff.   easy   e. accepting a discounted meal from a restaurant owner in your patrol area.

6. diff.   easy   f. accepting $10.00 at Christmas time from a businessman in your patrol area.

7. diff.   easy   g. discovering an open business establishment at night, and removing merchandise
for personal use.

8. diff.   easy   h. using your police badge or ID card to
gain free access to a movie theatre.

The questionnaires were administered in six police agencies
during a twelve-month period in 1975 and 1976. The sample
size was between 50 to 150 officers depending on the department size; a total of approximately 750 officers were questioned. The McCormack-Fishman Improbity Scale 1 asked
the respondents if, in terms of their own standards of honesty, it would be difficult or easy for them, as police officers,
to justify eight activities. In each activity, they were to circle
"difficult" or "easy" on the questionnaire. The random list-
ing of activities was reordered by the respondents according
to the level of seriousness they attached to each activity. For
example, 95% of the respondents in a department might
consider accepting a free cup of coffee as being easy to
justify as opposed to only 40% who might be able to justify
taking a $10 gift at Christmas time. In each of the six
departments the reordering of the eight activities was identical. The results from the activity easiest to justify (number 1)
to the most difficult to justify (number 8) are as follows:

1. accepting a free cup of coffee from a restaurant owner in
your patrol area

2. accepting a discounted meal from a restaurant owner in
your patrol area

3. accepting a free meal from a restaurant owner in your
patrol area

4. using your police badge or ID Badge to gain free access to
a movie theatre

5. accepting $10.00 at Christmas time from a businessman in
your patrol area

6. accepting gifts from a towing company for preferential treatment at accident scenes

7. discovering an open business establishment at night, and removing merchandise for personal use

8. accepting sums of money on a systematic basis to allow a gambler to operate

Although the reordering of the individual activities was identical in all six agencies surveyed, the mean number of respondents who selected one or more items as being easy to justify varied. Using the total survey population within a department, a score for the agency was determined (Fishman, 1978). For example, if the score for a department was 1.20, the score indicated that the respondents could easily justify accepting a free cup of coffee but found some difficulty accepting a discounted meal. A score of 3.40, however, would indicate that accepting free meals was easy for most officers in that department to justify and that some did not find it difficult to use their police badge for free access to a movie theatre.

The McCormack-Fishman Improbity Scale 2 used the same eight activities. Respondents were asked to indicate which of the activities would result in discipline if it became known to their immediate supervisors that respondents were engaging in them.

The reordering of the items in Scale 2 was identical to the reordering in Scale 1, and the mean scores by department, although not exactly identical, were similar for Scale 1 and Scale 2. Departments that had a higher improbity reading indicative of lower ethical awareness in terms of their own standards of honesty (Scale 1) also scored a high reading on Scale 2, which indicated a higher tolerance for unethical behavior by supervisors.

The McCormack-Fishman Scale 3 was developed later by the Project to determine at what level of observed improbus behavior would one police officer report that behavior. The same eight activities were listed, and respondents were asked to indicate whether they would report a fellow officer whom they observed engaging in them.

Preliminary data indicates that in police departments registering low levels of unethical activities, the tendency among officers *not to report* unethical behavior on the part of their peers is high.

Although further analysis of the data from the questionnaire is planned, the following theoretical precepts have emerged from the research:

1. A direct relationship exists between the consistency of enforcement of anti-corruption policy and the levels of ethical behavior with a police agency.

2. A reading on the McCormack-Fishman Improbity Scales of 3 or higher indicates that serious corrupt behavior by individuals or groups is being practiced and is being systematically performed.

3. Pro-active internal affairs procedures are essential in every department, because law enforcement personnel are reluctant to report the unethical activities of their peers.

II
Corruption Hazards, Indicators, and Procedures to Control

After the Anti-Corruption Management Project was established, the staff relied on the expertise developed over time by internal affairs units in a number of large urban police agencies. Most internal affairs units had developed manuals of procedures and guidelines for their investigators. One of the most sophisticated of these manuals was developed by the New York City Police Department (City of New York Police Department, 1975).

The Internal Affairs Division of the New York City Police Department viewed itself as a staff resource to subordinate commanders. In 1973, precinct commanders and other decentralized unit heads were given the responsibility and capability to command their units. The responsibility for eliminating corruption was among the newly delegated mandates, and each command was assigned a lieutenant to function as an integrity control officer who was directly responsible to the precinct commander. Precinct commanders were subject to removal if it became known to a higher department authority that systematic or conspiratorial corruption existed in the precinct.

The development of an internal affairs capability in precincts decentralized the New York City Police Department's anti-corruption efforts for the first time. The usual confusion that initially follows any major reorganization occurred, including a misunderstanding of the duties and responsibilities of the precincts, unclear reporting procedures, and an unspecified relationship between internal affairs personnel in precincts and personnel in the Internal Affairs Division.

To establish a concerted, systematized approach to the new anti-corruption program, the Internal Affairs Division developed a manual of procedures. It listed corruption-prone or hazardous situations which were to be carefully monitored by precinct integrity control officers. It specified places where officers could easily become involved in corrupt activities. One place, for example, was a traffic stop where police have low visibility. The manual also specified indicators of possible corruption like the excessive stopping of motorists in one place as compared to summons or arrest activity in another place. The manual recommended control methods like frequent on-site supervision and review of activity records by superior officers. It recommended also that policy be clear regarding selective enforcement and the issuing of warnings for violations of traffic laws. The potentially corrupt situations covered in the guidelines are quite specific and are reproduced in their entirety for possible adaptation by other agencies. Some local laws and ordinances may make some of the situations unique to New York. Generally, the material is *germane* to police work throughout the country. Simply reading this material will increase an administrator's awareness of potential corruption hazards and suggest some innovative control procedures.

The following material has been edited from a draft of a manual (City of New York Police Department, 1975) developed by the New York City Police Department.

BARS, GRILLS, CABARETS AND BOTTLE CLUBS

Hazard:

— the acceptance of money, gifts, free food and drinks by members of the department from owners and operators of bars and grills, cabarets and bottle clubs to overlook violations of the Alcoholic Beverage Control Law, the Health Code, Traffic Regulations, and Administrative Code.

— Police unofficially assisting owners and operators of premises in the maintenance of order.

Indicators of Problem:

Unexplained visits by department members to bars, grills, cabarets, and other licensed and unlicensed premises, indicated by:

— failure to notify the radio dispatcher of visit.

— failure to notify supervisor on patrol.

— no arrests, summonses, or other police action taken when necessary, and failure to make proper reports.

— improper or incomplete investigations of crimes occurring on or near premises.

— a specific pattern of visits to the premises by department members on and off duty.

— the presence of illegal parking in the vicinity without proper police action being taken.

Numerous complaints from the public alleging:

— disorderly premises.

— overcharging for meals, drinks and services.

— adulterated liquor and wine, especially adulterated champagne.

— credit cards lost or stolen from clothing checked in cloak rooms or from individuals on the premises.

— police cashing personal checks that subsequently are returned by banks due to insufficient funds.

— assaults on patrons by employees or persons on the premises.

— improper or no police action taken when police are summoned with complaint to premises for cause.

— taxicab drivers, hotel employees, and others bringing people to prearranged specific locations like bars, clubs and hotels for a fee.

— unlicensed premises (bottle clubs) selling alcoholic beverages.

— premises frequented by persons who are obviously narcotic addicts or prostitutes.

— without appropriate police action subsequently taken, individuals being injured in the vicinity of licensed premises under circumstances that might indicate that the injury occurred within the premises.

— receipt of written or verbal communications alleging an improper presence of police in the premises or alleging some police corruption.

— business being conducted during prohibited hours.

— through personal observations, premises are frequented by known gamblers or racketeers without intelligence reports having been received from patrol service units.

Follow-up inspections reveal that complaints, referred to other commands for action, are not being acted upon effectively.

Inspection of records reveals that cases resulting in arrests or summonses have an inordinately low conviction rate for some premises.

Procedures to Control:

"Routine" visits prohibited. Inspections should be conducted on a directed basis by the precinct commanding officer.

Commanding officer or executive officer should direct superior officers to make frequent observations of suspected premises and persons suspected of corrupt practices.

Information received from within the department and from the public should be verified.

Conduct personal interview of complainants, when deemed necessary.

Personally inspect and analyze department records to detect possible trends or patterns of police action in connection with premises under suspicion.

Carefully observe members of the department suspected of having a drinking problem that would cause them to become amenable to corruptive efforts by others.

Enforcement Policy:

Suspicious activity should be referred to proper department unit when summary arrest cannot be effected. Other agencies like the Fire Department, Department of Buildings, interested community groups, and elected officials should be requested to assist.

Accountability for Adherence:

Superior officers on patrol should make frequent observations. Roll call instructions should be used by the commanding officer to enunciate his policies. Periodic conferences should be held with patrol officers for both instruction and exchanges of information. The precinct commanding officer should use command discipline, charges and specifications, or in appropriate cases, prompt referral of complaints to the internal affairs unit. The commander should also visit owners and managers of premises, and make known to them his policy, request their cooperation, and advise them that an offer of a gratuity or other consideration to a public officer is a crime and the person making the offer is subject to arrest. He should seek the aid of the chaplain for members suspected of being alcoholics.

CONSTRUCTION SITES

Hazard:

— the acceptance or solicitation of money, gifts and building materials by police to overlook violations of the law pertaining to the regulation of construction.

Indicators of Problem:

— unexplained visits to construction sites by police while on and off duty.

— police observed placing building materials into department vehicles or into their own private vehicles.

— identifiable violations which create safety hazards for pedestrians or which impede traffic flow at construction sites apparently being overlooked by police.

— written or verbal complaints received from the public alleging violations at construction sites without proper police action being taken.

— complaints received from construction workers or site managers alleging excessive enforcement.

— unusual summons activity by a member of the department, followed by sudden inactivity.

Procedures to Control:

Direct written or verbal communications to site managers informing them of departmental policy and requesting their cooperation in enforcement. Advise them that the offer of a gratuity to a public officer is a crime and that the person making the offer is subject to arrest. Superior officers should make frequent observations of sites to insure adequate enforcement of pertinent laws and to observe the conduct of police observed at construction sites without sufficient reason for their presence.

Carefully examine summons and other records to detect signs of pressuring site managers by department members.

Inspect construction sites immediately upon receipt of complaints.

Enforcement Policy:

A policy of non-enforcement of regulations against building construction unless the conditions impede vehicular or pedestrian traffic, or affect the health and safety of the public. A superior officer should be present when summons is issued.

Accountability for Adherence:

Superior officers on patrol should make frequent observations of construction sites to determine that pertinent laws are being adequately enforced. Commanding officers should use roll calls to educate members of the service in present department policy. It is the responsibility of commanders to make their policies known to their subordinates in definite terms and to visit the superintendents in charge of construction sites to inform them of department policy and request their cooperation.

HOTELS AND RESTAURANTS

Hazards:

— the acceptance by police of free meals, free rooms, and Christmas gratuities from owners and operators of hotels and restaurants to overlook parking, health codes, administrative code violations and laws pertaining to public morals.

— police unofficially assisting owners and operators of these premises in maintaining order.

Indicators of Problem:

— unexplained visits to the premises by police on duty and off duty.

— receipt of written or oral complaints alleging members are obtaining free meals and rooms.

— observations of violations of laws inside and in the vicinity of the hotels and restaurants without adequate enforcement activity for correction.

— complaints from the public alleging violations of the liquor laws and the laws pertaining to gambling and prostitution that should have been discovered and reported by members of the service.

— complaints, especially those alleging improper police action, of assaults on the public by employees of hotels or restaurants.

— hotels and restaurants having a known policy of free for "man on post."

Procedures to Control:

Make independent observations of premises for an evaluation of any crime problems that may exist.

Direct observations to detect the furnishing of unwarranted police services.

Carefully examine reports on injured individuals and complaint reports, the origins of which may have been in a hotel or restaurant instead of the location where actually reported taking place.

Compare the findings revealed by observations of suspected premises with arrest reports and with the results of other completed investigations.

Disseminate current departmental policy to members and to the owners, managers, and employees of hotels and restaurants and request their cooperation. They should be advised that an offer of a gratuity to a public officer is a crime and that the person making the offer is subject to arrest.

Provide adequate sleeping facilities in the station house for police who need those facilities.

Enforcement Policy:

Intelligence reports should be submitted regarding suspected violations of laws concerning public morals. Traffic regulations should be strictly enforced.

Accountability for Adherence:

Superior officers on patrol should make frequent observations to determine if any particular restaurant is frequented by police who may be receiving free or discounted meals. Commanders should visit suspicious premises and in a face-to-face discussion clearly state department policy.

PARKING LOTS

Hazard:

— the acceptance by police of money, gifts, free parking privileges, and Christmas gratuities from the owners and operators of parking lots to overlook violations pertaining to their businesses.

Indicators of Problem:

— violations of traffic regulations and congested, vehicular traffic in the vicinity of the entrances to parking lots.

— parking of customers' automobiles on streets in violation of departmental regulations.

— deliberate inattention to violations by members on patrol.

— unexplained visits to the parking lots by police while on or off duty.

— written or verbal communications received alleging that police frequently observed overlooking violations.

— complaints from parking lot owners and employees that they are unnecessarily receiving summonses for borderline violations.

Procedures to Control:

Observe and inspect patrol supervisors to observe that laws concerning parking lots are being enforced fairly.

Inspect daily activity reports to detect unusual and suspicious trends of activity.

Frequent observations by commanders of persons and places susceptible to corruptive efforts.

Enforcement Policy:

Strict enforcement of the applicable laws concerning parking lots should be made when violations are creating inconvenience to the public or are a safety hazard.

Accountability for Adherence:

Superior officers on patrol are responsible that the laws pertaining to parking lots are properly enforced through observations and inspections. Commanders should use roll call instruction and training practices to insure that police on patrol know the precinct's policy concerning parking lots. Follow-up inspections should be used to determine whether policy is being followed. It is the commander's responsibility to visit parking lots and to outline clearly to owners and employees the policies of the department and to advise them that the offering of gratuities or other considerations is a crime and that the person making the offer is subject to arrest.

REPAIR SHOPS, GARAGES, TRUCKING COMPANIES

Hazard:

The acceptance by police of money, gifts, and free services from owners and operators of repair shops, garages, trucking companies, and vehicle rental companies to overlook violations of the laws pertaining to traffic regulations and to general business laws.

Indicators of Problem:

— double parking and parking on sidewalks in the vicinity of said businesses, without proper police action being taken.

— loading or unloading in non-loading zones resulting in the obstruction of sidewalks.

— streets or sidewalks being used as storage areas.

— major repairs, other than emergency repairs, being performed in the streets.

— receipt of numerous complaints about noise of trucks and cars, without any corrective action taken by patrol service units.

— written and oral communications received from the public alleging collusion between members of the command and the businesses.

— unexplained visits by members of the command on or off duty to the businesses.

— an inordinate number of rented automobiles recovered through arrests or recovered as abandoned, by specific members of the command. Arrest records could indicate a desire for rewards from the companies.

— complaints received from operators and owners of the businesses, alleging excessive harassment by members of the command.

Procedures to Control:

Direct superior officers to observe and inspect businesses frequently to ascertain that traffic regulations and general business laws are being properly enforced. Inspect department records to discern possible trends like a lack of summons activity.

Enforcement Policy:

Summons activity should ensure the safety and convenience of the public.

Accountability for Adherence:

Superior officers are responsible through inspections and supervision that members of patrol service units properly enforce the laws and regulations concerning car and truck businesses. Commanding officers should personally visit owners and operators to inform them of department and precinct policies and to request their cooperation. They should be informed that the offer of a gratuity or other considerations is a crime and that the person making the offer is subject to arrest. Commanding officers should use roll call instructions, conferences, and memos to instruct members of the command in precinct and department policy.

GYPSY OR UNLICENSED CABS

Hazard:

— the acceptance or solicitation by police of money and gifts from gypsy cab drivers and operators of livery car services to overlook violations of traffic regulations.

Indicators of Problem:

— stopping an inordinate number of gypsy cabs without arrests being made, summonses served, or adequate reporting made by members of the command.

— the receipt of a number of written or verbal communications from gypsy cab operators alleging harrassment by members of the command.

— rumors circulating within the command concerning the acceptance of bribes from gypsy cab operators, especially if they relate to specific members of the command.

— unexplained visits by police on and off duty to gypsy cab offices or garages.

— failure by patrol services to take corrective action concerning traffic conditions and unnecessary noise in the vicinity of gypsy cab offices and garages.

Procedures to Control:

Direct superior officers to observe and to supervise closely members of the command in the enforcement of regulations governing gypsy cabs.

Enforcement Policy:

Selective enforcement of traffic regulations should insure the public's safety.

Accountability for Adherence:

The commander should inform members of the command concerning precinct and departmental policy about gypsy cabs through roll call instructions, memos, and meetings. The commanding officer should use written and oral communications to owners and operators of gypsy cabs, especially to leaders in the industry, informing them of department policy and requesting their cooperation. They should also be informed that the offering of money, or other considerations is a crime and that the person offering bribes is subject to arrest.

TRAFFIC VIOLATIONS

Hazard:

— the acceptance or solicitation by police of money and gifts to overlook traffic violations.

Indicators of Problem:

— excessive stopping of motorists by police without comparable summons or arrest activity.

— serious traffic and safety conditions — illegal parking, street repairing of automobiles, sidewalk parking, and low enforcement activity — left uncorrected by department members.

— written and verbal complaints received from the public alleging non-enforcement of traffic regulations or alleging payment to police for special treatment.

— receipt of complaints alleging police officers attempted to extort money to overlook violations.

Procedures to Control:

Direct superior officers to observe places and persons in areas of traffic to insure adequate enforcement and to prevent corruptive practices.

Closely supervise members assigned to traffic control or parking enforcement duties.

Frequently inspect activity reports to discover possible corruptive practices.

Enforcement Policy:
An enforcement policy should be commensurate to the problem. Selective enforcement should ensure public safety. The indiscriminate issuance of summonses should be avoided, because it leads to abusive practices.

Accountability for Adherence:
To ensure compliance with department rules and regulations, superior officers on patrol should frequently observe members of the department enforcing traffic regulations. Commanding officers should use roll call instructions, memos, and meetings to instruct members in departmental and precinct policy regarding enforcement. Followup inspections should be made by commanders to ensure compliance.

TOW TRUCKS

Hazard:
— the acceptance or solicitation of money, gifts, and free services by members of the department to overlook violations of the laws governing tow trucks and to compensate police for referring operators of vehicles in accidents to specific towing companies.

Indicators of Problem:
— an inordinate percentage of towing business within the precinct being handled by a very few towing companies.
— tow truck operators violating traffice regulations without corrective action being taken by patrol officers.
— verbal or written complaints, received from the public alleging collusion between members of command and tow truck operators.
— members of command observed in possession of business cards of towing or body-and-fender repair companies.
— the receipt of a substantial number of written and verbal communications from tow truck operators alleging harassment by members of command.

Procedures to Control:
Superior officers on patrol should respond to the scene of all accidents requiring tow service.

Direct superior officers to frequently observe suspicious towing operations and suspected department members.

Initiate follow-up investigations of selected collisions involving a tow to determine any possible police corruption.

Distribute to motorists at accident scenes handout sheets describing laws pertaining to tows.

Enforcement Policy:

Strict, impartial enforcement of the laws and regulations pertaining to the tow truck industry should be maintained.

Accountability for Adherence:

Superior officers are responsible through observation and supervision to recognize and correct any possible corruptive practices to tow trucks. The commanding officer should visit tow truck concerns in his precinct to inform operators of the laws relating to bribery and request compliance with those laws. Operators should be informed that offering gratuities or other considerations is a crime and that the person making the offer is subject to arrest. The commanding officer is responsible that the members of his command are aware of present department policy.

PROSTITUTION

Hazard:

— the acceptance and solicitation of money and favors by police from prostitutes to overlook violations of the laws relating to prostitution and prostitution-related offenses.

Indicators of Problem:

— unnecessary familiarity with known prostitutes by police while on or off duty.

— failure of the uniformed patrol service to adequately control public nuisance conditions when prostitutes or pimps congregate on streets to actively solicit patrons or when hotels, massage parlors, bars, and apartments are apparently being used by prostitutes.

— the presence, on or off duty, of a member of the command not on police business, at locations frequented by known prostitutes.

— recurring arrests of the same prostitutes as a harassment technique by individual officers for reasons other than impartial law enforcement.

— written and verbal complaints from the public alleging collusion between members of the command and prostitutes.

Procedures to Control:
Observe frequently suspicious areas of prostitution, pimps, prostitutes, and police to determine if any corruption patterns exist.

Initiate follow-up inspections to determine what action has been taken by plainclothes units regarding information supplied to them by patrol officers.

Enforcement Policy:

Selective enforcement should be used to ensure public safety and to eliminate the public nuisance of prostitution.

Accountability for Adherence:

Superior officers on patrol should ensure that the department's policies regarding prostitution are adequately enforced. Commanding officers should indoctrinate members of their command in departmental and precinct policy relating to the enforcement of laws on prostitution. Commanding officers should also seek acceptance of their policies by hotel managers, bar owners, and owners of other businesses frequented by suspected or known prostitutes.

GAMBLING

Hazard:
— The acceptance or solicitation of money and gifts by members of the department from individuals involved in illegal gambling activities to overlook violations of laws regulating gambling.

Indicators of Problem:
— known gambling locations operating within the confines of the precinct without proper intelligence reports being submitted by members of the command.

— crowded parking conditions in the vicinity of suspected premises, especially during evening hours, that indicate possible organized card or dice games.

— large numbers of people entering a business establishment like a candy store, shoe shine parlor, or grocery store and leaving shortly thereafter without having made a purchase.

— numerous observations of known gamblers at specific locations.

— members of the command, while on or off duty, in the company of known gamblers or frequenting locations suspected of gambling activity.

— failure by patrol officers to correct public nuisance relating to gambling.

— the receipt of written and oral communications alleging that members of the command are permitting gambling to take place.

Procedures to Control:

Initiate frequent observations of individuals, locations, and members of the command suspected of being involved in corruption relating to gambling.

Direct superior officers to observe suspicious gambling locations frequently. Initiate follow-up inspections by the commanding officer to determine whether intelligence reports are being submitted for all suspected locations and persons within the command.

Accountability for Adherence:

The commanding officer is responsible through roll calls, training, memos, and conferences, that members of his command are aware of present department policy relating to the enforcement of gambling laws. The commanding officer should frequently inspect the departmental files to determine their completeness and accuracy concerning gambling conditions. The commanding officer is responsible for comparing gambling arrest reports with court affidavits to determine the accuracy of the reports and to investigate the loss of cases which appeared to be strong.

NARCOTICS

Hazards:

— prior to booking, the unlawful release of prisoners in exchange for money, narcotics, or other gifts.

— unwarranted dismissal of court cases after police consiracy with offenders.

— the withholding of contraband by police for private use, future sale, or the practice commonly known as "flaking" or placing evidence of a crime on a person who does not actually possess it.

Indicators:

— an arrest pattern by specific officers which indicates a concentration of arrests for loitering and narcotics trafficking by people waiting to buy or sell.

— repeated observations of police at locations frequented by narcotics users, especially when no other police business is occurring at those locations.

— despite the receipt of complaints, narcotic locations flourishing without proper police action being taken.

— a pattern of complaints by prisoners alleging that money, other valuables, and narcotics are missing after the suspects have been searched by police.

— a pattern of complaints that charge improper search and seizure.

— a pattern of allegations of evidence being placed on a supposedly innocent person to justify an arrest.

— an unusual number of court cases being dismissed because of incomplete or faulty court affidavits, poor testimony, or non-appearance of specific members of the department.

— members of the department spending money presumably in excess of their income.

— possible narcotic use by members indicated, in addition to the usual physical signs, by excessive requests for emergency leave; excessive sick report time (noting type of illness), neglect of personal appearance; constant fatigue; inadequate attention to duty; allegations or rumors of an individual's involvement with usage; unexplained disappearance from station house of property from personal lockers, vouchered property, and office equipment; and observation of a department member's associates.

Procedures to Control:

Closely supervise subordinates in the field to insure the proper handling of arrests and searches.

Establish strict procedures for searches and the recording of evidence. Immediate search in presence of station house supervisor and recording of evidence should be made. Supervisor should issue a receipt for evidence that the arresting officer can place in his memo book.

Hold frequent conferences with superior officers and community groups to obtain information related to suspected practices in narcotics enforcement.

Initiate frequent independent or parallel observations of narcotic locations and of suspected officers.

Frequently review individual records to determine suspicious trends in arrests, dispositions, and investigative results.

Train members in current departmental procedures and policies.

Hold periodic, unannounced locker inspections to discover the unlawful withholding of evidence or contraband.

Review all narcotic arrests by superior officers, especially cases that are dismissed in court.

Enforcement Policy:

Strict enforcement should be made of all laws pertaining to narcotics.

Accountability for Adherence:

Superior officers should be responsible for instituting all measures listed under *Procedures to Control.*

SABBATH LAW VIOLATIONS

Hazard:

— the acceptance or solicitation of money or gifts by members of the department to overlook Sabbath Law violations and violations of other laws pertaining to businesses open on Sundays.

Indicators of Problem:

— unexplained visits by on or off duty police to stores within a command.

— police observed placing packages into their private automobiles or into a department vehicle while on duty.

— police observed making systematic visits to numerous stores without cause.

— rumors or complaints against police concerning their actions in connection with violation of Sabbath Laws.

— suspected violations of alcoholic beverage control laws not being reported by members observed in grocery stores open on Sundays.

— complaints alleging violations of Sabbath Laws not being properly investigated.

Procedures to Control:

Frequently observe places and persons suspected of engaging in corruptive practices.

Make regular inspections of activity reports to detect unusual trends or patterns of activity.

Enforcement Policy:

Compliance should be made with the current complaint-oriented department policy concerning stores open for business on Sundays. Upon receiving first complaint, issue summons; after receiving second complaint, make arrest.

Accountability for Adherence:

Superior officers on patrol should make an immediate inquiry upon observing members of their command at business locations on Sundays, especially when no other police business is occurring at those locations.

Commanding officers should meet with store owners, merchants, managers, and trade association members to obtain information on results of present policy and to obtain information about the behavior of members of their command.

Commanding officers should use training to instruct members of their commands in current departmental policy.

Businessmen should be informed that the offer of a gratuity to a public officer is a crime and that the person making the offer is subject to arrest.

STREET VENDORS

Hazard:

— the acceptance or solicitation of money or merchandise by members of the department from street vendors to overlook violations of health codes, traffic regulations and regulations issued by consumer affairs agencies.

Indicators of Problem:

— police observed in unnecessary conversation with street vendors.

— observations of members, either on or off duty, receiving merchandise from peddlers.

— the failure of the patrol officers to adequately control the public nuisance caused by peddlers.

— complaints received from local merchants alleging failure to enforce regulations governing peddlers.

— the receipt of written or oral communications from street vendors concerning excessive harassment by members of the command.

Procedures to Control:

Closely supervise superior officers on patrol to determine that regulations governing peddlers are properly enforced.

Instruct members of the command about precinct policy and the use of command discipline for members found lax in the enforcement of laws and regulations.

Enforcement Policy:

Upon receiving initial complaint, issue summons; after

receiving second complaint, make arrest and take merchandise as evidence. Instant photography helps to establish identities of peddlers.

Accountability for Adherence:

Superior officers on patrol should implement measures listed under *Procedures to Control.* Commanding officers should conduct periodic follow-up inspections to ascertain that departmental policy is being followed.

GYPSY CONFIDENCE GAMES

Hazard:

— the acceptance or solicitation of money by members of the command from persons engaged in the operations of confidence games to overlook violations of the law pertaining to their illegal enterprises.

Indicators of Problem:

— numerous store-fronts occupied by gypsies who are conducting no apparent legitimate business.

— the unnecessary familiarity by members of the patrol services with gypsies.

— on and off duty members of the command not on official police business, observed making regular visits to gypsy store-fronts.

— receipt of written or verbal complaints from persons alleging that they have been victimized by gypsies and alleging that they have received inadequate police attention in regard to their complaints.

— numerous automobiles, especially those with out-of-state plates, (gypsies frequently utilize Alabama plates) parked illegally in front of locations used by gypsies, without proper police action being taken.

— the extensive distribution within the command of handbills advertising gypsy enterprises like fortune-telling and spiritual healing.

— numerous unlicensed gypsy flower vendors observed conducting business within the command.

Procedures To Control:

Initiate frequent observations by superior officers to determine if members of the command are unnecessarily involved with gypsies.

Enforcement Policy:

The commanding officer should attempt to discourage gypsies from establishing illegal business enterprises within his command. The commander can use strict enforcement of the parking regulations in the vicinity of gypsy store fronts and other businesses, can promptly investigate complaints of crime committed in gypsy businesses, and can request the assistance of police specialized in dealing with confidence games and pickpockets for persistent problems.

Accountability for Adherence:

The commander must insure that members of the command are aware of policies concerning "gypsies." Superior officers on patrol should through supervision, observation and inspection, insure that the commanding officer's policies are maintained.

PISTOL PERMITS

Hazard:

— the acceptance and solicitation of unauthorized fees by members of the command from the public to facilitate the processing and approval of pistol permit applications.

Indicators of Problem:

— applications issued and processed only by a specific member of the command.

— members of the command observed typing applications for citizens or observed assisting them in any unauthorized manner.

— numerous requests by pistol permit applicants to see a specific officer.

— the unwarranted rejection of completed applications by a member of the command claiming that they are incomplete or improperly prepared.

— the vast majority of investigations of applicants being conducted by a specific officer or by a select group of officers.

— incorrect and vague assessments made by sergeants of the amount of cash and valuables handled by businessmen requesting pistol permits.

Procedures to Control:

Applications should be available from the supervisor on duty in the stationhouse in order to circumvent restricted issuance by one specific individual at his convenience.

Station house supervisors should check applications for completeness.

All applicants should be fingerprinted by the station house officer.

Accountability for Adherence:

Commanding officers and superior officers should frequently spot check completed background investigations of applicants which have been conducted by other officers. Commanding officers should be responsible that written instructions have been issued to each applicant. These instructions should inform applicants how to complete the application and detail the applicant's rights and obligations as a pistol permit holder. Applicants should be advised that the offer of a gratuity or other considerations to a public officer is a crime and that the person making the offer is subject to arrest.

ADMINISTRATIVE CORRUPTION

Hazards:

— acceptance or solicitation of money or gifts by police in exchange for information from department records.

— acceptance of gratuities by police from other police for assignments within commands, days off, improper lost time credit.

— scheduling of court appearances by police for their days off.

Indicators of Problem:

— police spending money presumably in excess of their income.

— a pattern of court appearances or appearances before other agencies on scheduled days off.

— a pattern of overtime caused by police preparing forms and doing paper work at the end of tours of duty.

— a pattern of payments to only certain police for overtime, portal-to-portal travel, and night differential scales.

Procedures to Control:

— Select trustworthy members for care of time records.

— Frequently monitor night differential and overtime payment records.

— Frequently examine time records and vacation selections.

Accountability for Adherence:

Superior officers and station house supervisors are responsible for the careful examination of return roll calls, vacation requests, one day excusals, time records, lost time records, return dates, and night differential payments. Commanders and superior officers are also responsible for monitoring these records systematically.

CHRISTMAS GRATUITIES

Hazard:

— the acceptance or solicitation of money, gifts, free services by members of the department to overlook violations of law or for past services.

Indicators of Problem:

— affluence of police presumably in excess of their income.

— police entering stores, shops, and business offices during Christmas holidays without any apparent reason for being in the premises.

— receipt of written or verbal complaints from business people alleging solicitation of Christmas gratuities.

— presence of lists of business locations.

— police seen removing merchandise from police cars and placing it in private automobiles.

— clerical staff observed shopping in area of assignment while on meal period.

Procedures to Control:

Initiate frequent observations by superior officers on patrol of police at business locations and in the vincintiy of the station house.

Periodically examine radio cars.

Inform the public and the media through letters or handbills about gifts to police officers and request the public to report police who seek gratuities.

Use roll calls and unit training sessions to explain policy on Christmas gratuities.

Urge superior officers to question clerical staff returning to station house with packages that are obviously not for department use.

Enforcement Activity:

Strict enforcement of traffic and other regulations in vicinity of businesses susceptible to solicitation should be made.

Accountability for Adherence:

Superior officers are responsible through observations and supervision to recognize and correct any possible corruptive practices. Commanding officers should send to merchants written and verbal communications informing them of department policy and requesting their cooperation in enforcing policy. Commanders should address meetings of the Chamber of Commerce, businessmen's associations, church and fraternal organizations. They should enunciate department policy in concise, logical terms and solicit the cooperation of these groups. Every opportunity to address these groups during the year should be accepted. They should be informed that the offer of a gratuity or other considerations is a crime and that the person making the offer is subject to arrest.

III
The Media
and
Police Corruption

A police department which is unresponsive to pressures outside of it may prove to be ineffectual and may find itself in an environment where corruption can flourish. Usually, public sentiment about police will be reported in the local press and media. Consequently, the police administrator should establish positive relations and open lines of communication with the press and media. The following excerpt from a New York City Police Department Operations Order is an example of a positive approach to the media:

Subject: Cooperation with New Media

An informed public is essential to the maintenance of of a free society. In addition, the public is entitled, as a matter of right, to be informed on matters of public interest. Consequently, the highest degree of cooperation between the Department and the news media must be attained, consistent with established policy and procedure. We must be ever cautious, however, in striving for this high degree of cooperation, that information disclosed to the media in no way subverts the ends of justice or infringes upon individual rights to privacy, constitutional or otherwise.

Cynics argue that those who are corrupt or potentially corrupt obviously have an interest in diverting attention from their own improprieties. Honest police administrators who have failed to control corruption have no desire to call attention to their failure. But these explanations do not account for the silence of police leaders strongly committed to rooting out corruption or the silence of rank-and-file police personnel who themselves are honest.

Many police administrators fear the discovery and publicizing of police corruption by the media. In many cities, police are suspicious of, even hostile toward the media. In some areas, fears may be justified, but generally a cooperative attitude by police toward the media is a good approach. Under no circumstances should an administrator attempt to conceal corruption. To do so can be disastrous, as more than one administrator has discovered.

UNDERSTANDING THE MEDIA

One cannot assume that all representatives of the media are the same. Reporters and editors from newspapers, magazines, radio, and television each approach news in vastly different ways, and each is likely to report on the same story in various ways. The electronic media places great emphasis on the attention-getting aspects of an event but rarely offers in-depth reporting. In the print media, a story is likely to be covered in greater depth than on radio or television. Investigative reporting has recently become common particularly in the large cities. Investigative reporters, unlike the average reporter, are ususally assigned to a story for a long period of time and, not unlike the criminal investigator, will carefully explore every development of their investigation (Burnham, 1976).

Despite a generally antagonistic feeling among most police officers and administrators, the media is supportive of law enforcement, and analyses of media content indicate that most reporting is very favorable to the police. Unfortunately, one negative story can have detrimental and traumatic effects on a police department. Police often feel that stories, particularly those relating to corruption, are unfair, are frequently sensationalized, and do not present an objective view of law enforcement. The so-called "rotten apple" theory of corruption is frequently viewed with skepticism by reporters, especially when a department refuses to cooperate or provide information in a case.

The media has the responsibility of reporting news, and corruption is news. Most reporters are given inflexible deadlines for their stories and under pressure, they may overlook information or may fail to conduct thorough interviews. Reporters in the electronic media are particularly prone to emphasizing the sensational aspects of a story.

The manner in which reports of police corruption are revealed is likely to have an impact on the way reporters will write about corruption. The expose is probably the most troublesome type of story, and many administrators, probably to some degree correctly, argue that a reporter assigned to writing an expose is not unbiased. However, most exposes do not come as a surprise to administrators, and generally reporters offer them an opportunity to comment on what they are planning to expose in the media.

An officer arrested or charged with corrupt activities is a newsworthy subject. The reporter assigned to the story may or may not be familiar with the criminal justice system. On a large newspaper, the city desk editor assigns reporters to stories daily. The "police beat" on most newspapers is not usually viewed as a status assignment, and frequently the young, inexperienced reporters are assigned to this beat.

Although reporters in the United States are increasingly professional, college-educated individuals, very few journalism schools offer any comprehensive study of the criminal justice system. The average police reporter is probably a novice in understanding the complexities of law enforcement. Although police reporters have a duty to report all of the news, they are often unaware of the potential impact of a detrimental story, particularly an unfair or inaccurate one, upon the reputation of a police department or upon individual officers.

When a major story is broadcasted or published, a wire service like United Press International or the Associated Press may also assign reporters to cover the story. Although wire service reporters are generally more experienced than police reporters, they may not be familiar with the particular department involved or with its policies and procedures. These reporters may need background information from police administrators.

The impact that the news media can have on relations between police and the public is thought to be great, but it is difficult to determine the long-range effects of a detrimental story. Frequently, police react with anger to a story involving corruption. The news media attempts to report what is happening, and over-reaction or careless statements by police can be as harmful to a department as the story itself. The police administrator must understand the news media and be familiar with the reporters to whom he talks and with the kinds of stories he may expect.

WORKING WITH THE NEWS MEDIA

Working relationships with the news media should not be taken casually. Careful consideration must be given to what may appear to be minor details in responding to a reporter's inquiry. Personal appearance, location of the interview, the way of speaking and associates present at the interview should be considered.

A press conference should be handled differently than an individual interview. When a press release has been issued, an attempt should be made to anticipate questions from reporters. When working with the electronic media, an attempt should be made to learn what questions will be asked. An informed police administrator will usually not be surprised at a question. Especially at a press conference concerned with corruption, a police administrator should be able to present his position thoroughly and objectively; he must not mislead reporters or conceal information from them.

Most police administrators probably have developed good relationships with certain representatives of the news media, and those relationships, if they are to continue mandate full and accurate disclosure of newsworthy events. Some police tend to cooperate with reporters who are friendly and to ignore those reporters who ask detailed, probing questions. The administrator should make a conscious effort to be available to all reporters.

BEING INTERVIEWED

Some understanding of the process of an interview is important. Honesty in an interview is usually the best policy, and attempts to be less than honest can backfire. However, the way in which a question is answered can influence an audience. People communicate non-verbally, and facial expressions or a tone of voice can communicate more than what is said. Understanding the psychology of interviewing can be important, because a good reporter is skilled in interviewing techniques. As Gorden (1975, p.89) states, "Even the most potentially threatening information will be given an interviewer under the right circumstances." Frequently, an administrator is unable to provide all the information requested by a reporter, particularly when a case may still be under investigation, and although the administrator should remain honest in his replies to reporters' questions, he must use restraint in revealing information which he may legally not devulge.

Care should be taken in the choice of words used in interviews. Stock phrases like, "The case is still under investigation," may not satisfy reporters or the public, who may sense a cover-up. Instead, a police administrator can explain in detail what actions will be taken in an investigation and can promise that the results will be released.

When a department has initiated a corruption investigation, the administrator is in a better position with the media than when an investigation or allegation of corruption occurs outside of the department. When responding to an external investigation, the administrator must convince reporters that a thorough investigation of allegations is taking place. Frequently, reporters may fail to ask a question that is important, and when possible a police administrator should try to introduce important information rather than to simply respond to reporters' questions.

Before conducting a press conference or meeting reporters, the administrator should make every effort to prepare himself adequately by being fully briefed about what will be discussed. In a large department, the administrator usually depends on either oral or written reports from subordinates who may not be completely knowledgeable about all the specifics of a case. Those responsible for conducting an investigation of a case should be questioned in detail, and the administrator should make every attempt to become familiar with details that may be unclear. Ideally, a mock press conference, with members of the department acting as reporters, can be of immense value to an administrator.

During an interview or press conference, the administrator should control the pace of the questioning. Answering questions too hastily may result in slips-of-the-tongue and an appearance of nervousness. It is not unreasonable to take a moment to think about a response to a question. When possible, questions should be considered in chronological order to avoid confusion concerning the sequence of events.

TALKING ABOUT CORRUPTION

Police corruption is a controversial topic, and many police administrators cannot discuss it without becoming virtually enraged. Nevertheless, as Herman Goldstein (1975) states:

> Until recently, it has been almost impossible to generate open discussion of corruption by police themselves. If corruption was discussed at all, it was done privately, among officers who knew and trusted each other. Corruption was seldom referred to in police administration and law enforcement

texts. It was rarely covered in any depth in police training programs or discussed formally at meetings of police administrators. Most strikingly, administrators of some of the most corrupt police agencies have publicly denied the existence of a problem. When confronted with evidence of wrongdoing, they have de-emphasized the problem by dealing with the wrongdoers and claiming that they, like a few rotten apples, were exceptions in an otherwise clean barrel.

Today there is a greater willingness to discuss the problem. The session on police corruption at the 1973 meeting of the International Association of Chiefs of Police was among the most heavily attended of the entire conference. Articles on the subject are appearing in police journals. Several conferences have recently been held for the specific purpose of encouraging more open concern. But even at meetings called to discuss the problem, some participants try to divert attention from police corruption by insisting that it should be seen as only a part of the problem of corruption in the criminal justice system and society.

Cynics argue that those who are corrupt or potentially corrupt obviously have an interest in diverting attention from their own improprieties. Honest police administrators who have failed to control corruption have no desire to call attention to their failure. But these explanations do not account for the silence of police leaders strongly committed to rooting out corruption or the silence of rank-and-file police personnel who themselves are honest.

Unfortunately, no adequate definition of corruption or misconduct exists, and many police administrators have found themselves being criticized for tolerating behavior previously regarded as acceptable. Without being criticized in the media, police have accepted gratuities and discounts.

According to current research, attitudes toward these activities and other forms of minor misconduct vary from one section of the country to the other.

One mistake frequently made by administrators who talk about minor forms of corruption is denying that they exist. When it is common practice for police officers to eat free meals and when the practice is blatant and obvious, denial only leads reporters and observers to believe that the administrator is also lying about other problems. To state to reporters that the department actively investigates minor misconduct when it does not will not contribute to an atmosphere condusive to public support and may seriously threaten the credibility of the administrator. Most departments will conduct an investigation when a complaint is made, and internal investigations help to develop public confidence. Further, the public should be informed that private citizens can help a chief maintain a professional department. The administrator can ask the public to report acts of misconduct, explaining that misconduct could be reduced if those who offer free meals and services would refuse to do so. Many departments have virtually eliminated certain forms of misconduct, because of a strong policy and successful efforts to gain public cooperation.

Perhaps the most uncomfortable problem an administrator faces is discussing *serious* allegations of corruption. Responding to allegations of general corruption is much more difficult than responding to isolated cases of corruption. Although activities in narcotics and vice are inherently "corruption prone," the Project staff talked with many chiefs of police who absolutely denied any serious corruption, but the staff later found it almost commonly accepted in certain units. Consequently, caution must be taken when making a complete denial of "widespread corruption," which is a relative term that can be misunderstood. When corruption has been exposed, every effort should be made to inform the public that actions are being taken to combat it. Denying the existence of corruption is not a realistic approach to the problem. Usually admitting that corruption exists and outlining a program to deal with it will gain public support.

Since the Watergate scandals the public is suspicious of its elected and appointed public officials, and the police are as susceptible to media investigations as other officials. The administrator must not hesitate to confront allegations of corruption with honesty and objectivity. Corruption is an emotionally charged word which prompts unduly harsh responses from police, the media and the public. Effective cooperation with the media can turn scandal into positive reform.

SUMMARY — REACTING TO THE MEDIA

The following points should be kept in mind when reacting to the media:

— Be honest, and present a case clearly and in as much detail as possible without compromising ongoing investigations.

— Be thoroughly familiar with a particular case prior to meeting with reporters.

— Be cognizant of appearance, particularly when being interviewed for television.

— When a story is about to be revealed, try to announce it before it becomes an exclusive. If a press conference is needed, be prepared with a response, including what detailed actions will be taken by the department to investigate the case further and what is being done to see that similar cases will not occur again.

— Be selective in choosing your press spokesman. Utilize articulate, knowledgeable personnel who will accurately project your message.

— Get to know the various representatives of the media, develop rapport with them, and establish mutual lines of communication.

— Understand the technical and reporting differences between the electronic and the print media.

— Confront all issues openly and honestly.

The police administrator must recognize that the public has a right to know about police corruption. Police corruption is a matter of public interest; facts about it must be presented as accurately as possible. An established and impartial working relationship with the media helps an administrator to accurately report the facts of a case and informs the public that the administrator will not tolerate breaches of integrity in a department. Moreover, exposure in the media of arrests and disciplinary action for corrupt behavior will provide a deterrent to other officers who may be inclined towards corrupt activity. Secrecy, "cover-ups," and negative attitudes toward the media only diminish public confidence in the ability and effectiveness of the administration of the entire department. Conversely, frankness and honesty reflect an awareness of problems and a desire to make changes which will increase the effectiveness of the department and will simultaneously gain public confidence.

Policy
and
Program
Development

IV
Developing
an
Anti-Corruption
Policy

When a chief has defined, located, and measured corruption, he has the basic information necessary to formulate or devise an anti-corruption policy. After he decides on a policy, it becomes necessary to establish operations to put his policy into action.

When a strong anti-corruption management program exists, a chief can discuss corruption problems which affect the department. However, in many police departments, one utterance about corruption or misconduct is likely to be reported by newspapers, and a scandal can be created. Many of the police administrators interviewed by the Project staff said that they would like to do more than they did about problems of misconduct and corruption, but they felt that any action they took might be interpreted as indicating a major corruption problem instead of a minor one. Chiefs also stated other reasons for not initiating an aggressive anti-corruption policy. Some were concerned about the police union and police morale; others were worried about the reaction of public groups who support the police or who have an interest in perpetuating petty forms of corruption. However, one high ranking police officer said, "I know there's corruption, and so does the chief. But many of those involved are old friends, and after all, what's a few bucks here and there? We don't get paid all that much." This officer was earning more than $25,000 a year, and fortunately, he was representative of few of the police administrators interviewed by the Project staff.

For whatever reasons, it is usually easier for a chief to overlook minor forms of misconduct and to blame them on society. "Everyone else is doing it" was an extremely common response in departments where corrupt activities were flourishing. Unfortunately, the individual who most likely has the responsibility for eliminating corruption is a new chief, and he is frequently an outsider appointed as a reformer. It is difficult to say whether his job is easier or more difficult than the job of a chief appointed from within the department. It is certainly different.

Any new chief or incumbent administrator must realize that an effective program involves a total effort aimed at raising the consciousness of the department about corruption; it introduces measures to support high ethical conduct; and it identifies and deals with those who violate policies, rules and laws. An effective program cannot be short-ranged. It is a continuing effort which builds upon a succession of successfully completed goals.

The decision to develop an anti-corruption program may be based on many reasons, but it is likely to be precipitated by the discovery of corrupt activity by people outside of the department in the media or the political community. An administrator who is forced to react to potential scandal is in a weaker position than a chief who confronts corruption before it becomes a major public problem. Reaction to public allegations of corruption is likely to be viewed cynically by members of a department, because many may feel that the chief should do nothing except wait for scandal to dissipate.

Ideally, a decision to develop and implement an anti-corruption program should be made when a department is not receiving adverse publicity, when the administrator feels confident that he can control a corrupt situation, and, per-

haps most important, when subordinates who will administer
his programs can be trusted to be honest, objective, and loyal
to his programs.

DEVELOPING AN ANTI-CORRUPTION POLICY

To develop and implement an anti-corruption program, it
is necessary to develop a policy based upon an identification
of the indicators of activities listed in the previous chapter. It
is imperative that a new chief assess the level of corruption as
soon as possible after assuming office so that he can develop
and publicize his anti-corruption policy as quickly and
thoroughly as possible.

In most police departments, policies concerning misconduct and corruption, when stated in writing, are usually
general. Most policies or courses of action to be taken or not
taken in a given circumstance leave much to be desired.
Usually they are so vague and general that they discuss
virtually any kind of conduct which may be questionable.

SOME PROBLEMS IN DEVELOPING POLICY

For an anti-corruption policy to be viable and effective, it
must be realistic, manageable, and continually reinforced by
the police administrator. Undoubtedly, the most serious
forms of misconduct, particularly those which involve the
receipt of money or other forms of compensation for overlooking an illegal act, are definable. However, a number of
commonplace acts represent the most difficult activities for
which to establish policy. Some of these acts as determined
by the McCormack-Fishman Improbity Scales include: acceptance of free coffee. It is difficult to curtail the practice of
accepting a free cup of coffee when such a practice has been
traditional. However, several chiefs of police have established
successful policy which has usually been accomplished with a
specific statement of policy and a concerted effort with the
public. An example of one policy is provided later in this
chapter.

Although the general public and the business community
in particular must be informed of departmental policy regarding these activities, in most departments, the activities are

actual violations of written rules which are seldom enforced. To police administrators, they present problems in policy-making for a society in which many of these activities are acceptable. Of primary concern is whether or not an officer provides an extra service for a consideration. One administrator interviewed by the Project compared these kinds of activities to victimless crimes. A businessman offers a service to police for a variety of reasons, and usually they will not complain when the service is accepted. However, when a complaint is made by a civilian who observes and disapproves of these activities or by a businessman who feels as if police expect him to provide free or discounted goods or service, a police administrator must have a policy to deal with these complaints. Some suggestions made to the Project staff include the following:

— acceptance of free or discounted meals. Success in eliminating this activity usually depends upon the cooperation of those businesses which make it a practice to offer free or discounted meals.

— acceptance of discounts on merchandise, free uniform cleaning, and other services. Efforts to eliminate these activities can only be accomplished with support from the public and businesses.

— maintain a general policy regarding the dubious propriety of these activities but only selectively enforce it when a particular problem is brought to your attention. If an officer takes *unfair* or *extreme* advantage of these activities, an administrator should call the officer's attention to behavior which is not approved in the department.

— maintain a general policy and attempt to enforce it. Virtually all police interviewed by the Project indicated that maintaining a general policy was almost impossible. However, one chief maintained that a strict policy of enforcement has reduced minor misconduct significantly. He added that new officers were more likely to accept street policy than veteran officers. Although he felt it would take years to create an atmosphere in which all minor misconduct was eliminated, he maintained that a strict enforcement policy for minor violations deterred more serious acts.

— develop specific policies which permit certain activities

but which require the officer to sign a no-charge bill or receipt. The police administrator can then check the costs to the businessmen involved and can identify those officers who take advantage of the policy. Usually free coffee, discounted meals, and uniform-cleaning can be covered by specific policies.

Another problem mentioned frequently to Project members was the single acceptance of gifts, usually from a citizen who wished to express appreciation to a police officer. Most departments overlook the acceptance of individual gifts, but some require the officer to turn the gift into the department. Later, they are donated to charitable organizations or are used for department functions. When money is donated, it is added to the pension fund. One department indicated that it allows officers to accept individual gifts — after it approves a formal written request from an officer for permission to accept the reward.

Devolping policy to deal with minor misconduct is difficult and can be best accomplished by the chief in cooperation with an ethics committee which is representative of the department. The committee should make recommendations about minor misconduct to the chief, but ultimately the chief must determine the policy. The formation of an ethics committee may also be useful in handling unique situations and advising on policy. The committee might recommend that "letters of censure" be placed in an officer's personnel file as a mild form of discipline in cases of minor misconduct. The "letter" is a punishment only to the extent that an offending officer perceives it as punishment and not just another bureaucratic "piece of paper." If an offending officer is to be deterred, he must know that a "letter of censure" in his file may effect a future promotion or assignment adversely.

SERIOUS MISCONDUCT AND CORRUPTION

Serious kinds of misconduct and corruption should also be governed through specific policies. A major problem occurs, however, with personnel in specialized units who may be expected to perform acts which are inconsistent with department policy. Undercover officers may "buy" narcotics or may establish a newsstand to "sell" pornographic material. The formation of policy should take into account the illegal activities of narcotics and vice officers. The phrases — "except in the performance of duty and necessary to the objectives of the department" or "without permission of the Chief of Police" — are frequently used as disclaimers in anti-corruption policies.

EXAMPLES OF POLICIES

The Project staff examined a number of manuals outlining procedures and policies in police departments, and the following material has been prepared as a guideline for the development of policy:

> Corrupt or improper practice, which offense is committed where a member of a police force 1. fails properly to account for, or to make a prompt and true return of, any money or property received by him in the course of his duty, or 2. in his capacity as a member of the force and without the consent of the chief officer of police or the police authority, directly or indirectly solicits or receives any gratuity, present, subscription or testimonial, or 3. places himself under a pecuniary obligation to any person in such a manner as might affect his properly carrying out his duties as a member of the force, or 4. improperly uses, or attempts to use, his position as a member of the force for his private advantage, or 5. in his capacity as a member of the force and without the consent of chief officer of police, writes, signs or gives any testimonial of character or other recommendation with the object of obtaining employment for any person or of supporting an application for the grant of a licence of any kind. (Police Foundation, 1965).

Consequently it is a violation of department policy:

— to accept money, other objects of value, or any other type of compensation from individuals or entities for police services rendered without due authorization of a supervisory officer.

— to enter while on or off duty stadiums, theatres, sports arenas, or any other place where public spectacles are being held, without paying admisssion.

— to accept meals, lodging, transportation or any other benefit or facility from labor unions, business management groups or others involved in labor negotiations.

— to become involved in any business operation, especially licit, that may reflect detrimentally on the service or on the morality or reputation of the department.

— to use or employ outside influences to obtain transfers, promotions, or any other benefits.

— to solicit or accept a loan or guarantee for a loan from individuals suspected of illegal activities or with police records.

— to seek, accept, or agree to accept bribes, money, gifts, or any other object in exchange for overlooking illegal activities.

— to possess, sell, or buy any illegal narcotics, except those obtained as evidence in the course of discharging one's duties.

— to swear or subscribe to any document changing or falsifying evidence.

— to publicize or deliver, without due authorization, official documents, lists or reports in the possession of the police.

— to publicly or privately solicit money or any object of value from any individual or entity.

One police department includes ethical standards training in its curriculum. In thinking about anti-corruption, a police chief and his ethics committee might want to consider the following canon of ethics for adoption:

> The law enforcement officer, representing government, bears the responsibility of maintaining, in his own conduct, the honor and integrity of all government institutions. He shall, therefore, guard against placing himself in a position in which any person can

expect special consideration or in which the public can reasonably assume that special consideration is being given. Thus, he should be firm in refusing gifts, favors, or gratuities, large or small, which can, in the public mind, be interpreted as capable of influencing his judgment in the discharge of duties (Davis, 1974).

Another police department in a large city, after a major scandal, established some policies, by an internal board of ethics. The policies, divided into subjects or kinds of corruption and guidelines may serve as prototypes for other agencies:

— *Subject:* soliciting discounts from stores or entering theaters or sports arenas free of charge by police.

— *Guideline:* It is unethical *without exception* for a member of the department, based solely on his being a member of the department, to solicit or accept any discount on merchandise or services or to solicit or accept entry without fee to any place of entertainment.

However, a distinction is made between attending community-sponsored affairs or city-sponsored events for police or firefighters at a stadium and routinely using a shield for free admission. Members of the department should attend events in an official capacity to improve community relations or may as police officers, attend functions where they are to be honored by a sports team and the public. However, use by a member of the department of his official position to gain special favors is demeaning to the police service and is unethical.

— *Subject:* gifts given to members of the department.

— *Guideline:* When considering the ethical propriety of accepting a gift the following aspects of the gift-giving situation should be examined and considered carefully: 1. What is the value of the gift? 2. What is the intent of the donor? And 3. What is the intent of the recipient?

Valuable gifts like money, savings bonds, or expensive watches, if they are given in appreciation or recognition of police service, should not be accepted at any time by members of the department. In some cases, however, a gift or reward may be reviewed by an ethics committee and, if approved by the police chief, may be accepted. The acceptance of gifts of little value like inexpensive plaques, pen and pencil sets, or favors given to everyone attending a function, is not considered unethical.

The intent of the donor and the doner's expectations regarding the nature of his relationship with recipient members of the department is an important consideration. If the donor's conduct or demeanor indicates that he may expect special treatment from members of the department as a result of his gift, the gift may not be accepted regardless of its value. Members of the department must be prudent in deciding whether to accept or decline a gift. Although, the intentions of a donor clearly do not involve influencing the members's official conduct, the gift must be declined if others believe that the doner is influencing official conduct. The appearance of corruption has the same negative effect upon the image of the department as does actual corruption. All facts about the purpose of the gift must be publicly known before the gift is clearly acceptable.

The intent of the recipient of the gift should also be considered. The intentions of police officers would not be questioned if while attending a large public dinner they accepted an inexpensive gift given to everyone present. Intentions could be suspect, however, if a valuable gift were given to one policer officer; or if over a period of time, inexpensive gifts were routinely given to him; or if any gift, regardless of its value, were given a police officer by someone with whom that officer has official contact.

When a gift is inexpensive, the member of the department should use personal judgment in accepting or declining the gift. When a gift is unique or valuable, the member should not accept it without a prior ruling by an ethics committee and, when warranted, approval of the police chief. When an expensive or unique gift is given to a member at an official ceremony, or when refusal would embarrass the donor, the gift should be accepted in a way that indicates that the acceptance is on behalf of the department. Guidance from an ethics committee should then be sought to determine the disposition of the gift. When prior knowledge exists of any intended presentation by a person or organization to a member of the service, prior advice should be obtained from an ethics committee. When warranted, approval of the police chief will also be necessary.

No exceptions to these guidelines are to be made during the Christmas season. Members of the department must be especially careful to avoid accepting or appearing to solicit gifts during the holiday season.

Members of the department must always use good judgment in accepting gifts. When doubt exists, the gift should not be accepted without a prior ruling of an ethics committee.

— *Subject:* Attendance at dinners, buffets and ceremonies sponsored by commercial interests when members of the department are invited free of charge.

— *Guideline:* Free attendance at dinners and other ceremonies involves an ethical question which has application to other public employees. One ethics committee in New York City recently stated:

> . . . We do not believe it improper, for example, if a city employee, at the invitation of one doing business with the city, is a guest at an annual public affairs organization such as those composed of representatives of business, labor, the news media or groups of a civic, charitable, professional or community nature; or if a city employee is a guest at ceremonies or functions sponsored or encouraged by the city as a matter of public policy, such as those involving housing, education, legislation, government administration or matters of a civic, charitable, professional or community nature. (City of New York, 1973).

A police chief, with the advice of his ethics committee can, using the quoted statement, determine under what specific circumstances it is ethical for members of the department to attend dinners and ceremonies free of charge. Attendance without charge at these affairs must be for the purpose of improving community relations or police-citizen understanding. Under no circumstances should a member of the department accept free admission as a personal favor or as a gratuity offered because of his official position or duties. The difference must clearly be made between attending functions in an official capacity for the benefit of the department and attending ceremonies solely in the furtherance of personal interests. When a member of the department places himself in a position where his private interests conflict with his official duties, his position is unethical.

If a question exists regarding the acceptance of invitations, the guidance of an ethics committee should be sought. Pertinent material in patrol guides and in Rules and Procedures should also be consulted.

— *Subject:* the acceptance of a cup of coffee.

— *Guideline:* It is recognized and accepted in most societies that the offer of a cup of coffee to another person in a private home is a social courtesy. Refusal may, under certain instances, be taken as an insult by a host or hostess. The value of the acceptance of a hospitality like a free cup of coffee must be weighted against the damage done to the spirit of community relations when an offer of hospitality is refused.

In certain instances, refusal to accept the hospitality offered to a police officer may hurt communications between the police officer and members of the community he serves. Under these circumstances, the acceptance of a cup of coffee would be proper or ethical.

Sometimes a police officer is on sick calls awaiting an ambulance or awaiting a medical examiner or coroner. When an officer is legitimately detained for a period of time in a private home on official police business, and a host or hostess offers a cup of coffee and sandwich freely as a token of sociability, courtesy should be considered in responding. However, a police officer must never leave his assigned post or linger unnecessarily merely to be sociable. In public places, a police officer must never spend time accepting hospitality.

Restaurant owners offering free cups of coffee or meals, newspaper vendors offering free newspapers, storekeepers offering free cigarettes or magazines, cannot be considered in the same way as individuals displaying a sense of hospitality in a private home. Usually any "free" offer is made by store owners with the expectation that special consideration will be returned by the police officer for the "free" cup of coffee. In a few instances, an owner may make an offer without any expectations of a return favor by the officer. However, the appearance of an owner's expectations is perceived by the public, and when appearances to the general public are improper, the involved behavior is prohibited.

Consequently, a police officer may not accept any free or discounted items from any merchant when the same items are not given to the general public. Not only must the behavior of police be free of impropriety, but the public must perceive the police officer to be beyond reproach.

Once an ethics committee is established within a department and is accepted as the arbitrator and policy-making group within the agency, officers can request rulings on the propriety of a variety of situations. Several are reproduced below:

Facts: A police officer was assigned to duties which included corrdinating some activities of an athletic league sponsored by the department. The officer was interested in becoming a part-owner of a sporting goods store located outside this city. Part of the officer's duties included processing requests by the league for sports equipment. He also had prepared a large order for sporting equipment processed through another youth agency. The officer has no apparent influence concerning the actual placement of orders for sporting goods from any vendor.

Ruling: The ethics committee determined that it would be unethical for the officer to become part-owner in a sporting goods store while assigned to duties with the athletic league.

Explanation: Members of the city government doing business with other city agencies are subject to legal restrictions. Although the sporting goods stores did not do business with the city, if the police officer became a part-owner of the store, the potential for conflict-of-interest was great. The committee also felt that the appearance of the officer's part-ownership, even to the most casual observer, would be unfavorable to the officer and the department.

Facts: A community group wanted to hold a testimonial for a local commander who would be presented with a plaque for outstanding efforts in promoting community relations. The group wanted to invite a number of police officers and superiors from other local commands to attend the dinner free of charge. The ethics committee was asked to determine if attendance at the dinner and acceptance of the plaque would be ethical for the commander and if other police could attend the testimonial free of charge.

Ruling: The ethics committee determined that it would not be unethical for the commander to attend the dinner and accept the plaque. It also determined that, under the circumstances, it would not be unethical for other invited police to attend the testimonial free of charge.

Explanation: Acceptance of the invitation and plaque by the commander is not unethical if no other gift is offered and no attempt is made by the sponsoring organization to use the commander's presence for a purpose that would compromise his integrity or would place the department in an unfavorable position.

Regarding the acceptance of free admission by other invited officers, the ethics committee believed that the fundamental question was whether the attendance by police would improve community relations. The committee felt attendance would help relations and was therefore not unethical.

When a chief has carefully assessed all available data and has decided what his anti-corruption policy will be, it must be communicated to the public and to the department as soon as possible. The following are some ways by which policy may be communicated:

— issue press releases and convene conferences.

— formulate, publish, and distribute a code of ethics. A code of ethics may be printed on posters or on small cards which may be carried in an officer's memo pad. The posters can be displayed conspicuously in police facilities. The code can also be printed on a handbill addressed to merchants; it should state the department's policy concerning rewards and gratuities. The handbill can be distributed to members of the business community individually or via regular meetings of business groups and the local chamber of commerce.

— develop a list of prohibited activities and publish it in department regulations or as an operations order.

— develop a statement or chapter for the published regulations of the department. Address the problem of corruption and outline the procedures to follow when reporting corruption internally.

— create an ethics committee or an ethical review panel, consisting of a ranking officer, a member of the clergy, an attorney, preferably from within police ranks, and a member of the department whose rank is comparable to that of the officer whose action is to be reviewed. The committee would not serve as a disciplinary trial panel, but would make judgments concerning the ethics of a particular practice or situation. Members of the department having doubts about potentially corrupt behavior or actions should submit their concerns for review. The rulings of the committee should be published and distributed to all other members of the department.

— develop ethical training programs.

V
Developing
an
Anti-Corruption
Program

Having determined what his department anti-corruption policy will be and having communicated that policy to the public and to his personnel, the chief must now develop a program to implement and enforce his policy.

PLANNING AND DESIGN

The planning and design of an ethical standards program should involve as many individuals concerned with anti-corruption as possible. All ranks should be represented. Representatives of police unions and line organizations should be included. Those who will be directly affected by anti-corruption policy — internal affairs personnel, department administrators, social prosecutors and district attorneys — should be consulted, and during the planning period all available information from these groups should be discussed. At all times, the chief should make clear that the positive aspects of the program far overshadow its repressive aspects.

In large departments, efforts should be made to use sub-groups like precinct integrity officers and field internal affairs officers to work on specific aspects of the problem. When discussing specific problems like traffic tickets or illegal parking the administrator should remember that there is likely to be denial and hostility. He should note that misconduct and corruption take many forms, and he should illustrate some of the activities which do exist and are well known. The process of defining potentially corrupt activities will vary from one department to another, but probably few departments are totally devoid of corruption. The corruption varies in degree and scope for each department.

The planning committee should meet frequently, at least once a week, and necessary staff work should be completed prior to the meeting. After two or three meetings, an agenda should be developed to enable the group to work on specific issues. Although no amount of time necessary to develop and design a plan should be predetermined, care should be taken to insure that the group does not become lost in details and non-productivity. Rumors about the committee's work will be circulating within the department, and they will create a negative backlash due to misunderstanding. Backlash may be avoided by de-mystifying the work of the committee via some form of explanatory internal communication. In large departments, the committee may require more than six months to complete its assignment, but rarely should more time be necessary.

A final draft of the program should be reviewed by administrators, unit heads, supervisors, and a representative group of first line personnel. They should all be asked for their comments prior to implementation of the program. When a final draft is presented, it should be specific. It should delineate the purpose of the new program, the ways it will function, and the disciplinary actions for violations. Emphasis should be placed on the preventive nature of the program. The program should not be retroactive; investigations should not begin of activities which were commonplace prior to implementation, unless of course, they were violations of the law.

The program should include any organizational changes to be made, the role of training and education, including curricula, and a statement of goals to be achieved. Finally, responsibility for each aspect of the plan should be delegated to specific personnel. When specialized units are affected, the plan should clarify the reasons for specifically addressing members of these units. If, for example, an officer is required to take a polygraph examination prior to assignment to a vice unit or internal affairs, he should be able to learn why the department makes the requirement.

Because an anti-corruption program is likely to be controversial, some consideration should be given to how and when it will be released. Care also should be taken in word usage; avoid using words like "corruption" for minor forms of misconduct. Copies of the anti-corruption program, including the department's definitions of corruption, and the program's underlying rationale should be distributed to the news media and to the general public. The chief should be willing to meet with reporters to explain that the program is an effort to address what may be a *potential* problem of corruption. The chief should point out that positive action of the program will help maintain the high quality of the department. The chief is assuming that a major scandal is not going to be revealed immediately but is willing to admit that corruption may be a problem, and the program is his way of attacking the problem.

COOPERATION AND THE ROLE OF SUBORDINATES

The chief administrator of the program cannot enforce it, except in small departments. He must depend upon subordinates to supervise policies and programs. The sensitive and controversial nature of corruption makes it difficult to find administrators who are willing to assume responsibility for an anti-corruption program. Sometimes those administrators who are willing to volunteer may not be best suited to supervise the program. The individual selected to supervise an anti-corruption program must have the complete trust of the chief. He must be willing to accept the "flak" that goes with the position, and he should be accepted by the rank-and-file as an individual who is fair but firm.

The role of the individual responsible for implementing and administering the program is multi-faceted. In many departments these responsibilities are assigned to the head of the internal affairs unit. Such an assignment is not always wise, because the individual responsible for investigating corruption does not usually have the confidence of the patrol force, and cooperation and acceptance by the rank-and-file are vital to the success of an anti-corruption program. The focus of an anti-corruption program should be on prevention, and the individual responsible for the program must be able to interact with commanders of all units and have the authority to instigate necessary changes. Consequently, a deputy chief or high ranking administrator should be given the primary responsibility for implementing an anti-corruption program. He must have the complete support of the chief, and this support must be communicated to all members of the department.

As most administrators know, mandating a policy is no guarantee that all subordinates will obey that policy. Because an effective program must have the cooperation of subordinates, first line supervisors are extremely important to an anti-corruption program, because they are usually close to problems. However, because first line supervisors are also close to line officers, supervisors may be reluctant to take action which will place them in a bad light with subordinates. Enlisting the cooperation of supervisors may be more difficult than it might seem. Although responsibility for motivating first line supervisors generally rests with the unit commander, commanders may be reluctant to cooperate, because a unit commander's main responsibility is to provide the public with effective police services. Initially, an anti-corruption program may have a negative impact on the morale and performance of subordinates. Morale problems can usually be quickly overcome, particularly when new policies are clearly stated and enforced and when actions of unit commanders are supported by the chief. If the anti-corruption program results in the poor performance of subordinates, staff conferences should be held frequently to insure that policies are being enforced uniformly. One unit commander should not charge an individual with a violation which another commander has handled with a reprimand.

Units heads and supervisors in specialized units represent another problem, because they usually work closely together and are reluctant to jeopardize good performance in their specialized crime area to eliminate what some supervisors view as minor forms of misconduct. Particular attention should be given to specialized units to ensure that they are complying with department policy.

The acceptance of policy by subordinates and their co-operation in developing and subsequently implementing an anti-corruption program is essential. The involvement of line personnel in developing the program gives all members of the department a proprietary interest in it and should serve as a positive factor when the program is to be implemented.

EXTERNAL INFLUENCES

An anti-corruption program may come in conflict with interests outside of the police department, because as Sherman (1977) notes:

> The power of established politicians, the attitudes of the general public, and the policies of the news media may seem well beyond the police administrator's sphere of influence. Both police and social scientists generally assume that these elements of the political environment constrain the policies of the police administrator and are hardly subject to his control. Accordingly, the political culture defines the "zone of indifference" within which police administrators are free to act as they see fit (Wilson, 1968). However, the possibility of changing the political environment of police corruption has rarely been acknowledged.

When a chief raises the subject of corruption any number of external forces may react. The chief should inform the other governmental officials in his jurisdiction, like the mayor, the city manager, and the city council, of his anti-corruption program and its underlying rationale. These officials should also be informed about the development of the program, although ideally they should have been consulted in planning the program. Because many forms of misconduct involve businesses, it is likely that pressure will be exerted by commercial interests to curtail various aspects of the plan. A chief can expect resistance to a program from licensed premises, construction sites, businesses where illegal parking is prevalent, and firms which occasionally depend on the department for special favors.

A chief must be willing to hear from businesses complaints that officers are enforcing laws that were previously unenforced. He will probably receive requests to remove individuals from certain positions and "special requests" for preferential treatment. Once the administrator deviates from his stated program by granting special requests, he is vulnerable to severe criticism from subordinates, and his program is likely to fail. Adequate planning should reduce the number of complaints that arise, and consideration should be given to a department's response to complaints.

External pressures are a potential threat, and most administrators are well aware that political influence is a threat to the most professional department. When a compromise has to be made, it should be made during the developmental stage and prior to the implementation of the anti-corruption program. Compromises can be handled in a way which will maintain the integrity of the department. For example, if a decision is made not to enforce nuisance laws, it must be made clear to business people who will benefit from non-enforcement that no member of the department is entitled to a gratuity or gift for overlooking violations of nuisance laws.

The chief should also make every effort to enlist the aid of the public and citizens' groups in helping his anti-corruption program to succeed. Indeed, were it not for the larceny in the hearts of some citizens and some police, corruption would be virtually non- existent.

*Program
Implementation*

VI
Implementing the Anti-Corruption Program: Planned Change

To implement anti-corruption policy, a chief may use one or more of the following change strategies:
1. Rational-Empirical
2. Power-Coercive
3. Normative-Re-educative (Chin and Benne, 1969).

Underlying the Rational-Empirical strategy is the philosophy that employees will rationally do what is in their best interest. To effect change, one merely justifies the change by convincing employees that the change is in their best interest. A chief may state that because police officers strive to be considered as professionals, it is therefore in the best interest of police to perform their duties professionally. Corruption of course would prevent police from attaining professionalism.

The Power-Coercive strategy basically utilizes one's formal

authority to force the acceptance of change. A chief has the necessary power and influence to compel others to accept, willingly or unwillingly, a specific change. He can issue a directive stating his policy towards corruption and can stress his power to manipulate rewards and punishments regarding the acceptance of and compliance with his policy. A chief should be wary of this method of change, because it is probably the most ineffective over a long period of time.

A chief should not institute so many control procedures that the performance of his department is curtailed. The chief's foremost goal is to serve the needs of the community, and with overly strict management methods, service to the community will no doubt suffer.

Probably the most effective approach to long-term change is the "Normative-Re-educative" strategy which considers employees in a more comprehensive manner than the other two strategies do. The "Normative-Re-educative" approach utilizes many behavioral research findings about employees in organizations. Through a process of collaboration and participation, an effective, long-term change in the behavior of employees can be made. In chapter seven, Project Star provides an example of the "Normative-Re-educative" strategy for police recruits.

A chief utilizing the "Normative-Re-educative" strategy would involve as many of his employees at all ranks as possible in formulating a corruption policy and implementing it. The philosophical rationale behind the "Normative-Re-educative" strategy is described as follows:

> Since the imaginitave and influential research of Lewin (1948), most students of organizational behavior have come to accept that a person's participation in setting a goal increases the likelihood that he will act to insure that the goal is met. Presumably, when the follower has participated in determining what is to be done, he should understand and agree that a certain course of action is necessary and proper. In this participation, some quite high-level needs on the part of the follower are involved. He exercises some power and he has an opportunity to express

himself and his abilities. Ideally, there is voluntary implementation through this participation and determination. (Hampton, et. al., 1973, p. 153)

Making changes is a dynamic process. The adoption of an overall strategy of change should not preclude the use of any or all of the strategies described. As situations in a police department change, so can the use of strategies. A chief may initially use one strategy, and when it has served its purpose, he may resort to another strategy. A chief may initially adopt a "Power-Coercive" strategy which can result in disequilibrium among departmental members. The chief may then use a "Normative-Re-educative" strategy.

Each new chief faces unique situations when he assumes command. He may have been hired from another part of the country or from another department. A new chief who has been promoted through the ranks has an advantage of intimately knowing the department, its procedures, and its problems. His knowledge of departmental personnel should enable him to select people of honesty and integrity to help develop and implement an anti-corruption program. However, his main disadvantage would be his prior relationships with members of the department which can create professional rivalry for the new chief's attention. The new chief hired from another department will not have problems with prior relationships and can be more objective and independent. He will however lack a detailed knowledge of the department, its internal functioning, and its personnel.

ORGANIZATIONAL CONSIDERATIONS

Although no single organizational structure would appear to be completely effective in curtailing misconduct or corruption, observations by the Project's staff of numerous police departments indicate several criteria which must be present if a department is to be successful in its anti-corruption efforts. These criteria include:

— positive leadership and a strong commitment by the chief administrator to the elimination of corruption.

— a department relatively free from pervasive political

influence.

— authority and responsibility for anti-corruption efforts placed appropriately and clearly defined, for each level within the organization.

— clearly defined policies and procedures.

— an effective internal affairs unit.

POSITIVE LEADERSHIP

Effective leadership is acknowledged as a vital resource for corruption control, and formerly corrupt departments have succeeded in re-establishing integrity under the guidance of effective and forceful leaders. Virtually all administrators interviewed by the Project's staff maintained that strong, positive leadership by the chief is the key component in an effective anti-corruption management program. Leadership requires action as well as statements, and the administrator must make every effort to show by example and support that his policies are important to him. In departments where corruption has been a problem, the Project found many statements by the chief administrator against corruption, but these were generally not followed by decisive action and support of individuals who were attempting to adhere to policies. In these departments punishment of individuals who were involved in corrupt acts was relatively light. Few departments actually dismiss individuals for corruption, although a survey conducted by the Project indicated that in 1974 ten of twenty-nine responding departments dismissed at least one individual for corrupt activities.

To some extent, leadership to initiate anti-corruption efforts is likely to be met with hostility by subordinates, partially due to the occupational "code" of law enforcement. Like many other professions, police emphasize the importance of keeping and handling problems within their organization. However, it is virtually impossible to keep a police corruption investigation quiet. When a scandal occurs, the chief is frequently placed on the defensive by line organizations and external forces that do not want an investigation revealed. The chief must make every effort to maintain or regain the initiative, by consistently stressing the importance of a positive approach to anti-corruption management.

A department with a reputation for misconduct or corruption represents a major challenge for the chief, whether he is selected from within the department or is hired from another department. Because many challenges face a new chief, the problem of corruption may be overlooked or deferred during the early days of his administration. However, a new chief must recognize that failure to take an early position on corruption will make it increasingly difficult to attack the problem later. Some administrators maintain that an attack against corruption can only be effective during the first month of a new administration.

POLITICAL INFLUENCE

Pervasive political influence can virtually destroy an anti-corruption effort. However, it is impossible and undesirable to eliminate politics from a department. Because most chiefs report to an elected official, they ultimately are responsible to the public. Nevertheless, responsibility for managing the police department must rest with the chief administrator, and when external, political influences dictate his decisions, the confidence of the police and the public in his authority is diminished.

Primarily political influences intrude upon police administration when politicians ask that certain laws or action be overlooked, that assignment and promotion of personnel be influenced. In some departments, political influences appear to be used as reasons for not acting against corruption. The chief who claims that he cannot act against corruption because of political pressures is in great trouble, because there is no record of politicians ever having accepted responsibility for corruption in a police department. A chief cannot allow his authority to be threatened by political pressures. When it became known that high-ranking New York City administrators were aware of corruption problems and chose not to do anything about them, the Police Commissioner was replaced when the corruption had been exposed.

AUTHORITY AND RESPONSIBILITY

Although police departments publicly claim that they adhere to good management principles, many departments are administered by a chief. As one supervisor said to the Project's staff, "I have all the responsibility and none of the authority." Actually, it is rare for a supervisor to hold responsibility for subordinates, and rarely is a supervisor disciplined for the negative actions of subordinates, even when a consistent pattern of negative behavior exists. Although problems occur when responsibility is assigned to subordinates, it represents the only effective way of developing maximum involvement in anti-corruption efforts. The Knapp Commission concluded:

> Whatever its obvious hazards, vesting primary responsibility for all but the most serious corruption investigations in the commands concerned appears to be the most rational way for the Police Department to deal with the problem on more than an emergency basis. (Knapp, 1973, p. 216)

In a speech to a group of his commanders, Patrick Murphy, former Police Commissioner of New York, attempted to remove the unspoken rule that corruption is the responsibility of headquarters squads:

> It will be my policy to increase significantly your authority with a view to achieving greater effectiveness and efficiency. In return, you can be expected to be held to greater accountability for your exercise of direction and control. The law provides that each of you serves above the level of captain at my pleasure. It is my responsibility to remove from rank anyone among you who cannot, or will not, meet the high standards of the executive level. (Brown, 1972, p. 47)

Murphy assigned responsibility to all members of the department, particularly first line supervisors. Failure to take action against corrupt activity frequently resulted in disciplinary action against all of those in a chain of command. Recognizing that control over a large number of subordinates made it difficult for many supervisors to adequately manage personnel. Murphy was also successful in promoting a large number of sergeants who as supervisors acquired control and responsibility. Emphasis was placed on career paths, and efforts were made to "upgrade" the performance and responsibilities of supervisors.

The approach of the Los Angeles Police Department is similar to Murphy's, although Los Angeles has a longer history of anti-corruption efforts which have become operational within the department. Emphasis on the authority and responsibility of supervisors and command level officers provides a positive approach to anti-corruption efforts, and it has enhanced Los Angeles' reputation for professionalism.

Placing responsibility necessitates a clear definition of activities, areas for responsibility, and actions which must be taken. Certain acts like excessively arresting traffic violators, can be handled administratively, and others, like bribery will require further investigation and preferral of charges. To everyone who is assigned responsibilities, a chief must clearly define what the limits of their authority are.

POLICIES AND PROCEDURES

> Important in any administration are the policy guidelines which the leaders establish. If they are clear, relatively unambiguous, and if they deal with important matters, the energies of those in the organization can be directed and their achievement evaluated. Absent those virtues, the organization is left with expediency as its major determinant of approved conduct. (Brown, 1972, p.43)

Although the subject of policy has been discussed previously, it should be stressed that no organization can be administered effectively without clear policy. Ideally, policies should be published and disseminated to all members of a department. In those departments with corruption problems, the Project found that adequate policy statements were generally unavailable and were frequently vague.

The procedures of anti-corruption management require careful planning. Frequently, the Project found that the decision to develop an anti-corruption management program lacked adequate planning. A procedures manual should detail what actions all individuals involved in a particular event are responsible for taking. Those areas of action which are handled by supervisors or command officers should be distinguished from those areas handled by an internal affairs unit, which generally investigates more serious cases. Clear procedures lessen the probability of error in investigation, serve to insure uniform standards of application, and foster public confidence in a department's ability to maintain a high level of integrity. However, planning is crucial to the development of adequate procedures, and without it, an anti-corruption program will be ineffective.

INTERNAL AFFAIRS UNITS

Although the responsibility for an effective anti-corruption management program should rest with each member of a department, special attention should be given to the importance of the internal affairs unit. Deputy Superintendent Mitchell Ware of the Chicago Police Department has stated:

> Since the police executive cannot be everywhere at all times watching all subordinates, he or she must have an organizational unit which will keep its pulse on the department and report back, as to when and where potential or actual problem areas lie. If the police executive does not know where the trouble spots are, or why they have formed, he or she will not be able to develop methods and procedures for eliminating those malignancies. (Ware, 1977)

The size and functions of internal affairs units vary according to departmental size. Most departments with more than a hundred sworn personnel utilize an internal affairs or inspection unit; the larger the department, the higher the ratio of internal affairs investigators to sworn personnel. However, no correlation seems to exist between the number of complaints received by an internal affairs unit and the number of personnel assigned to that unit. Consequently, no indicator exists by which a chief can determine what the size of an internal affairs unit should be. Interviews by the Project staff with administrators indicated that the number of individuals assigned to internal affairs investigations is generally based on several variables, including:

— the number of complaints received.

— the number of cases handled.

— the responsibilities of the unit, since some units are also responsible for inspections.

— the nature of the misconduct or corruption problem.

In most departments, the commanding officer of the internal affairs unit reports directly to the chief; in some cases he reports to a deputy chief. Direct reporting was viewed by most administrators as important as a means of determining problems quickly and as a way of displaying support of the unit.

The following descriptions of the internal affairs units of the Los Angeles and New York City Police Departments provide a view of the organizational and procedural features of the units.

INTERNAL AFFAIRS DIVISION (LOS ANGELES)

The approach of the Los Angeles Police Department to internal affairs is based upon a well-established procedure that has been developed during a number of years. The Internal Affairs Division consists of 62 sworn personnel and 22 civilian clerical positions. Figure 1 indicates the number of personnel assigned by rank.

The entire Department consists of 7,525 sworn personnel, and the ratio of personnel in internal affairs to those in the Department is 1:110. If civilians are added to the personnel in the Department, the ratio is 1:148.

All complaints or allegations of misconduct, including anonymous complaints, are investigated by the Department. Complaints are received and accepted at any police facility, the Internal Affairs Division, external agencies like the prosecutor's office, or from the Board of Police Commissioners.

Any complaint received must be referred to the Internal Affairs Division which decides what unit will handle the complaint. When a complaint is referred back to a command for investigation, the commanding officer of the unit will conduct an investigation and prepare a report with conclusions and recommendations based upon the allegations and findings.

FIGURE I

PERSONNEL BY RANK
IN INTERNAL AFFAIRS DIVISION
OF THE LOS ANGELES POLICE DEPARTMENT

Commander	1
Captain	2
Lieutenant	6
Sergeant	44
Police Officer	9
Civilian (Clerical)	22
Total	84

Source: Los Angeles Police Department Questionnaire and site visit report by the Anti-Corruption Project.

The report must include a paragraph entitled, "Administrative Insight," under which the perceived reason why the violation occurred is given. Also suggested are what measures can be taken to correct the condition and to prevent its recurrence.

The commanding officer's recommendations are reviewed by officers senior to him. They must agree or disagree with the recommendations. All material is finally received by the Commander of the Internal Affairs Division who reports directly to the Chief.

Complaints are classified as:
— sustained
— not sustained
— unfounded
— finding of misconduct not based on complaint

When a complaint is sustained, the Internal Affairs Division Commander will evaluate the complaint to see whether police action violated policy and whether disciplinary action is consistent with previous punishments. The Commander's evaluation serves to maintain uniform standards of discipline while allowing him to consider extenuating circumstances or other factors in a case.

Because the first line supervisor has been given the primary responsibility for preventing misconduct, he or she is assigned to investigate most complaints involving a member in the unit.

All investigative interviews are taped, and sometimes an officer may be advised to resign as an option. In 1974, 13 officers and 23 civilians resigned or retired while disciplinary action was pending.

As a result of an agreement with the Police Protective League, which represents the officers, a polygraph may be used in an investigation. The complainant, however, must agree to undergo a polygraph examination before the officer is expected to do so. When a complainant agrees to undergo a polygraph examination, the officer is virtually mandated to do the same if requested by the Department's administration. The results of the polygraph are admissible in a department trial.

Polygraph examinations are also given to all officers assigned to Administrative Vice, Administrative Narcotics and the Intelligence Divisions.

Sworn personnel are assigned to the Internal Affairs Division for two years. The assignment is not viewed as a career job, but as one which contributes toward career development. According to those interviewed by the Project, there are more applicants for positions in the Internal Affairs Division than there are positions to be filled.

An officer may be reprimanded or suspended for one to twenty-two working days without a trial if all parties involved in the complaint agree to this punishment. For serious cases which may involve longer suspensions, a hearing is held before the Board of Rights. The Board of Rights can recommend a suspension of one to six months, a reprimand, or a dismissal. The Chief of Police makes the final determination of the complaint, based upon the Board's recommendations. The Chief may lower a penalty but cannot increase it.

The high level of integrity of the Los Angeles Police Department, which is acknowledged by police administrators throughout the country, is attributable largely to the efforts of former Chief William H. Parker, according to Chief Edward Davis and other members of the department. Parker's establishment of a strong Internal Affairs Division is viewed as a first step in the elimination of corruption and misconduct. The importance of a strong executive and management team is also viewed as being crucial to anti-corruption efforts. In addition Section 202 of the Los Angeles City Charter provides job security and insures that no member of the Police Department can be removed except for cause.

The *Manual of the Los Angeles Police Department* (1973) defines misconduct as:

— the commission of a criminal offense.

— the neglect of duty.

— the violation of departmental policies, rules, or procedures.

— conduct which may tend to reflect unfavorably upon the employee or upon the department.

The Law Enforcement Code of Ethics is adopted as a general standard of conduct by the Department, and specific areas of ethics are defined in detail. For example, integrity is discussed as follows:

> The public demands that the integrity of its law enforcement officers be above reproach, and the dishonesty of a single officer may impair public confidence and cast suspicion upon the entire department. Succumbing to even minor temptations can be the genesis of a malignancy which may ultimately destroy an individual's effectiveness and may contribute to the corruption of countless others. An of-

ficer must scrupulously avoid any conduct which might compromise the integrity of himself, his fellow officers, or the department.

INTERNAL AFFAIRS DIVISION (NEW YORK CITY)

In New York City, approaches to internal affairs have undergone significant changes since 1970. The New York City Police Department consists of 25,000 sworn personnel, and the Internal Affairs Division consists of 121 sworn personnel and 11 civilians. The ratio of employees in internal affairs to those in the Department is 1:70. Including civilians, the ratio is 1:90.

Before 1970, the functions of internal affairs in the Department was decentralized to the extent that each large operational unit or bureau maintained a Field Internal Affairs Unit which reported directly to the head of its respective unit or bureau.

FIGURE 2

PERSONNEL BY RANK IN
INTERNAL AFFAIRS DIVISION OF
THE NEW YORK CITY POLICE DEPARTMENT

Assistant Chief	1
Inspector	1
Deputy Inspector	2
Captain	18
Lieutenant	58
Sergeants	148
Detectives	42
Police Officers	114
Total	384

Source: New York City Police Department Questionnaire and Site Visit Report

All complaints or allegations of serious misconduct or corruption must be referred to the Internal Affairs Division. Complaints may be accepted through any facility by any member of the Department, including the officer on the beat who is obliged to accept a complaint from a citizen. Complaints are also received from other sources like district attorneys and the Office of the Special Prosecutor.

All calls and complaints to the Internal Affairs Division are recorded, then evaluated for seriousness. The commanding officer of the Internal Affairs Division determines whether or not a case will be investigated by the individual command, a Field Internal Affairs Unit, or the central unit. A complaint is categorized in one of three ways:

— full investigation
— investigation
— minor investigation

A report must be returned within four months on a major investigation; within sixty days on a regular investigation; and within ten days on a minor investigation. Minor investigations are usually conducted by an individual command, and a disposition of the case is sent to the Internal Affairs Division.

A staff supervisory section is responsible for inspecting Field Internal Affairs Units and assuring compliance with policies and procedures in investigations.

First line supervisors have a prime responsibility for anti-corruption efforts. Commanding officers have the option of instituting command discipline or "company punishment" for other offenses not involving corruption. Officers are purposefully given responsibility at operational levels with authority to discipline subordinates.

The Department also has several programs to identify and eliminate corruption. The Field Associate Program uses officers who confidentially report both corrupt and exemplary activities to a central unit. A Field Test Program involves such activities as having a citizen give a wallet to an officer to see what action he takes. The Ethical Awareness Program involves training designed to confront difficult problems like peer pressure.

Assignment to the Internal Affairs Division is voluntary, and most officers remain with the unit for two to three years.

However, a number of investigators and supervisors have been assigned to the unit for more than ten years.

An officer charged with an offense receives a departmental trial at which criminal charges are not made. The trial commissioner recommends punishment, from minor discipline to dismissal, to the Police Commissioner.

Observers of the New York City Police Department note that dramatic changes have occurred since 1970 and the beginning of a major corruption investigation. Much of the success in the Department's anti-corruption efforts are a result of reorganization, and the development of effective policies and procedures.

OUTSIDE CONSULTANTS

One tactic that should be given serious consideration by a newly appointed chief of police is the utilization of an outside consulting firm to assess the ethical levels of personnel in an agency. The services of the consulting firm are for the confidential use of the chief in assessing the *general* corruption levels within the department. They are not used to obtain evidence of specific acts of corruption by individual officers. The Project found that in some field testing programs an apparent ambiguity existed about the use of information provided by outside consultants. Although field testing techniques do not necessarily involve entrapment, individual violators were disciplined despite the *purported* intent of using consultants to assess general ethical standards within a department. Although recognizing the importance of field testing, the Project recommends that testing be conducted by outside consultants who will be objective in their assessments but who will also protect the confidentiality of the subjects being tested. As a result, the police administrator will be able to quietly assess the results of anti-corruption efforts without violating the rights of individual police.

FIELD ASSOCIATES PROGRAMS

Field associates programs were established to covertly break what one writer has called the closed fraternity of police:

> Initiation of a police officer into the conspiracy of
> silence may begin shortly after he enters a depart-
> ment. New police officers are screened by practi-
> tioners of the art of corruption to determine whether
> the newcomers should be allowed to partake in the
> rewards of corruption. If a rookie is not acceptable,
> those actively involved in corruption do not fear
> exposure, because an honest officer learns that he
> will face trouble if he raises questions about a situa-
> tion which has existed for years. (Beigel, 1977)

In field associates programs, selected recruits and veterans
of an agency obtain information concerning corrupt activities
of their peers (McCarthy, 1976). These programs have the
support of the Anti-Corruption Management Project. Project
researchers found that reporting fellow officers was a common practice within particular police departments. These departments had reputations of above average integrity and had
apparently consistently functioned on a highly ethical basis.
In many agencies, however, the practice of reporting one's
peers for corrupt activities is unknown. In a number of departments, police officers have engaged in systematic burglaries. These activities, although common knowledge to
many fellow officers, were never reported. An administrator
must be able to protect a department against burglaries and
other criminal activities. The most effective way of doing so,
noting that it is a short term solution to the problem of corruption, is a field associates program.

To be effective, a field associates program should be well
publicized internally, and all officers, other than regular field
associates, should be encouraged to participate. Once the
credibility of a department is established regarding its determination to end corruption and once its firm and *objective*
approach to discipline becomes known, more and more officers will begin to accept the ethical philosophy of the police
administrators. The Project found that most police officers
interviewed by researchers would prefer to work in an environment free of corruption or compromise. In the absence of

that environment, field associates are essential to an administrator's anti-corruption efforts.

IMPLEMENTING THE PLAN

The written ethical standards plan should be put into effect on a specific date, and the procedures outlined in it should take effect immediately. Although there is likely to be some negative feeling toward the plan, the chief should again be willing to meet with representatives of the police union and other groups who were involved in the planning process.

Most important is the need for continuous follow up and support of the plan. Many officers will view the plan as a reform effort that will soon end. The chief should constantly seek responses of officers to the plan and should identify those areas where progress is being made and where it is lacking. Ideally, a way to evaluate the plan will have been established to determine its effectiveness. Establishing objectives is helpful in evaluating progress. Ways of determining and measuring levels of misconduct and corruption have been discussed, and they should be useful in maintaining a check on progress.

As he daily supports the plan, the chief should at every opportunity commend those members of the department who are making a conscious effort to support it.

ENFORCING POLICY

Although the emphasis of an ethical standards plan is on prevention, some police will continue to violate rules and laws. Swift action to identify these individuals is crucial, and sanctions should be indicators to everyone that unethical conduct will not be tolerated. A sanction should be consistent with the violation. One officer interviewed by the Project staff noted that loss of a day's pay would not deter him from accepting gifts and free meals, because their value was much higher than a day's pay and because the probability of being caught twice was minimal. The attitudes of officers like this one must be considered in determining punishments, and individuals who continue to violate policy after being sanc-

tioned once should be severely punished for subsequent offenses. Of course, the chief must recognize that each situation is unique and that he must consider all of the variables in
a situation when enforcing his plan. Some administrators
maintain that the best deterrent is a strong example. Others
maintain that leniency is important. Ultimately, the chief
must decide how his plan is administered, but his decision
should be made first in the interests of the department and
second in the interests of individuals.

The chief must also act against supervisors who fail to
support the plan. He can discipline them through reprimand,
reassignment, preferring of charges, reduction in rank, or
other administrative sanctions. A supervisor is responsible for
the conduct of those people assigned to him, and when
breaches of integrity occur, action should and must be taken
against supervisors who subsequently are responsible for dis-
ciplining their subordinates.

VII
Training

Discussion in a training program of topics related to ethical standards, the problem of corruption, and the officer's role in combating corruption is important for recruits and experienced police officers. Unfortunately, little is known about the causal and psychological factors which involve people in corrupt activities. Only recently has a concerted effort been made to establish training courses to examine corruption problems. Perhaps the most popular form of training is known as "ethical awareness," a practical, realistic program designed to address corruption as a form of socialization in police work. Officers are confronted with simulated situations involving a decision-making process. The program is viewed by many police administrators as more effective than a series of lectures warning the officers of the evils and dangers of corruption.

Some police administrators argue that ethical standards cannot be taught but are a part of one's personality. (Shealy,

1976) However, research conducted on behavior modification indicates that corrupt activity may be part of the socialization process in many police departments. (Bahn, 1976) A review of training curricula in several police departments reveals great differences in content and style. Those programs which *appear* to be most effective (no data presently available proves effectiveness conclusively) are those which use role-playing or simulation to confront the police with actual situations in which he or she may become involved. An effective training program will specifically address those problems of corruption that a department is experiencing.

CURRICULUM DEVELOPMENT

Preparation of curricula designed to address corruption should focus on 1. recruit training, 2. in-service training, and 3. supervisory and management training. Courses in each of these kinds of training should address the specific problems of each group. A good curriculum is based upon research, an understanding of police operations, and the integration of practical exercises in the training process.

In addition to library research, an attempt should be made to study and identify specific problems which can be included in specific courses. It is important to be familiar with those kinds of misconduct which are common, particulary those kinds that will not be eliminated by training. Training is not likely to stop police from accepting free coffee, free meals, discounts, and a number of other activities which commonly occur in many departments. These activities should be addressed, but great care must be taken in discussing them. An instructor who states that free coffee or meals will not be tolerated, when in fact they are, only harms his own credibility. Recruits are faced with having to determine just what is "tolerated" when assigned to the street. An instructor might more realistically explain the realities by emphasizing that such activities are violations of departmental rules and policies, if they are, and stress the ethical responsibilities of professionalism. It is easy for a recruit to make a commitment in a classroom but is much more difficult on patrol to refuse a cup of coffee when confronted with peer pressure to do so. Understanding the operations of patrol and the pressures placed upon recruits will aid in developing effective curricula.

Ideally, the curriculum will include practical exercises which require students to make decisions in a variety of situations. The exercises work well with recruits, in-service personnel, and supervisors.

RECRUIT TRAINING

The number of courses and hours devoted to ethical standards and training will vary with the length of the curricula. At least four hours should be devoted to ethics, misconduct and corruption. Ideally, ethical standards will also be discussed throughout the curriculum, as is done in the agent training program of the Federal Bureau of Investigation and other federal agencies. When a department has numerous problems of misconduct or corruption, the number of hours devoted to training in these areas should be increased. The following courses are suggested for a basic recruit curriculum:

Departmental Policies and Procedures — Ethical Standards. This course should be a general review of policies and procedures, focusing on the expectations and responsibilities of the police officer. Policies and procedures serve as guides but do not cover all kinds of corruption. Discussion should emphasize the importance of professionalization.

Historical and Social Aspects of Police Corruption. Few police departments of any size have not been subject at one time to the problems of corruption. This course should explore the historical roots of corruption in policing and in society, emphasizing the impact on police departments and individuals, particularly as that impact affects public confidence. Discussion should focus on the ways by which corruption is introduced and can grow in a department.

The Psychosocial Costs of Police Corruption. This course should explore the pervasive influences of misconduct and corruption. The factors like indebtedness, temptation, peer pressure, and group socialization which cause a breakdown in ethical standards should be explored in depth. Recruits should be encouraged to identify and explore what they believe are factors contributing to police corruption.

Practical Exercises. Utilizing simulation, game-theory, and role-playing as teaching approaches, this course confronts students with making difficult decisions in situations that are likely to occur on the street. The instructor should help the class to develop adequate decisions which are consistent with the unique characteristics, policies, and procedures of the department.

IN-SERVICE TRAINING

An experienced officer is likely to be very resistant to a training program which emphasizes ethical standards. Frequently, however, he is representative of the group most in need of a realistic approach to corruption. The number of hours devoted to in-service training will again depend upon the unique characteristics and identified problems of the department. Lectures appear to have very little impact on in-service personnel, and an intensive training seminar with a small group is probably the most effective teaching approach. The chief of police or his representative should be involved in some aspect of training for in-service personnel, because misunderstandings of departmental policies are likely to occur with this group. The chief should explicitly state which activities will not be tolerated, keeping in mind that failure to enforce policies creates confusion and mistrust. There are distinct disadvantages to using training academy instructors or internal affairs personnel as the only lecturers, for the average patrol officer is likely to feel that the academy instructor is "not in touch with reality" and the internal affairs officer does not represent the street officer. When possible, a seminar approach should be used in the following suggested courses:

Ethics. This course should be taught by a trained group leader and should explore the various aspects of the police role as they relate to ethic standards. Ideally, a session should last between two and four hours, and every attempt should be made to raise controversial issues like accepted illegal practices, group solidarity, community acceptance, and the relevance of policies and procedures in combating problems of misconduct and corruption.

The Investigation of Misconduct and the Role of the Internal Affairs Unit. This course should include a brief lecture by the chief of police or his representative, followed by an extensive question and answer period. The tendency of the audience will be to avoid controversy, and the chief would be wise to mention controversial issues in order to draw the students into a discussion.

Practical Exercise. This course would be similar to the Practical Exercise given recruits.

SUPERVISORY AND MANAGEMENT TRAINING

The effectiveness of an anti-corruption program depends upon supervisors and management personnel. If they are not committed to the program, all of the efforts of the chief administrator will be in vain. Therefore, a police department wanting to rid itself of corruption must emphasize the training of supervisors and managers. Again, the chief administrator must communicate his views and specify what is expected in the drive to control misconduct and corruption. The following lectures should be included in a training syllabus:

Ethical Standards — Problem Areas. The lecture should identify simply those activities which are or are thought to be problems within the department. When possible, the results of research, patterns, or trends should be discussed. The primary emphasis of this lecture is to identify that misconduct and corruption which supervisors and managers are to address. Because many students will be skeptical or distrustful of any allegations, it is very important to explain why and how problems were identified. A lecturer should not say, for example, that police officers are accepting gifts; this allegation should be substantiated.

The Supervisor's Role in Combating Misconduct and Possible Corrupt Activities. This lecture should focus on the techniques, investigative approaches, and procedures for identifying, eliminating, and controlling misconduct and corruption. Since a supervisor has the primary responsibility for identifying and eliminating corrupt activities, instruction should help to heighten the supervisor's anti-corruption skills. The roles of the internal affairs unit and its procedures should be discussed. Again, a realistic approach must be taken, and students must clearly understand the policies of the department.

Practical Exercise. The practical exercise should include written problems. The supervisor must evaluate the information given and decide what actions would be necessary. Role-playing situations should emphasize the relationship between the supervisor and his or her subordinate in dealing with situations involving misconduct, including allegations of misconduct against another officer or supervisor.

PROJECT STAR

Project Star (California Commission, 1973) is an innovative and well-researched method for developing police training programs. The project was funded by the Law Enforcement Assistance Administration and developed for the California Police Officer Standards and Training by the American Justice Institute. The program is based on a study of the desired outcomes of police training. The initial survey of some 1,500 state and local law enforcement agencies posed several interesting questions. What do police officers actually do? What do police administrators and the public expect of police? What kind of training is needed to insure that those desired expectations are met? Once the desired behavior was identified, the researchers began program development, and as a result, a comprehensive training program for entry level police officers was developed. This program can be replicated in other jurisdictions with minor modifications for local conditions. What makes it valuable to anti-corruption management researchers is its segment on ethical awareness training.

The ethical awareness training module is entitled, "Displaying Objectivity and Professional Ethics." This module was developed to involve the recruit totally in moral and ethical decision-making through discussion, role-playing, interviews, and field work. The focus of this experience is to have recruits face and make decisions on important ethical issues before they actually confront those issues on the street.

Three basic orientations will ultimately effect one's moral or ethical decision-making. These orientations are important for a police officer to understand, because they will make the hard ethical decisions easier for some and make the rationalization of corruption easier for others.

The Relativist Orientation. People who are relativists will find the ethical principles of law enforcement very difficult to internalize. Their point of reference is the self:

> Each person determines for himself what contributes to his greatest happiness and acts accordingly. His only purpose in furthering the happiness of others is to further his own. In other words, the relativist views things from the perspective of 'What's in it for me? (California Commission, 1973).

It would seem that individuals with a relativist orientation would be least desirable as police officers because of the inconsistencies between their personalities and the personal long-term sacrifices demanded of a police officer.

The Utilitarian Orientation. People who are categorized as utilitarians have a healthy respect for their own happiness while being aware of and wishing to contribute to the welfare and happiness of others. Their desire to contribute to the welfare of others is raised to a duty upon entering the sphere of public or private service in the professions of medicine, law, religion, law enforcement, and politics:

> Utilitarianism has been widely used in political and large-scale social reforms where the focus was on revamping superficial and temporary causes of unhappiness . . . (California Commission, 1973).

The Absolutist Orientation. The absolutist theory, departing from the pleasure principle of the relativists and utilitarians, holds that the primary consideration is not the happiness or unhappiness produced by an action or any of its consequences, but on the nature of the action itself.

The same act is always right or wrong for everybody under the same physical or psychological conditions and there are acts which are always wrong under all conditions (California Commission, 1973).

In a homogeneous population with a similar sense of basic values and expectations, the absolutist orientation can result in a very legal professional style of law enforcement; each individual would be treated the same, and problems of corruption would be minimal. The contrast between this legal style of policing and the political, utilitarian orientation is clear. The latter not only recognizes individual differences but is tolerant and supportive of it. Since police usually have a utilitarian orientation, one can expect that they will tend to bend rules not only for citizens but for themselves.

Project Star also introduces the concept of the police officer as a model citizen. It indicates that an officer's private and professional life must be above reproach and must come as close to being ethically ideal as possible. A lecture-discussion is introduced entitled, "What I Do on my own Time is my own Business." This discussion illustrates how limits are imposed on even the personal lives of officers by their professional code of ethics. It is useful in this part of the training program to have an experienced officer discuss some of the real ethical issues he has had to face and how he personally resolved them. It is important in the discussion to address the gray areas of ethical conduct and to destroy all the rationalizations which tend to support unethical responses. Effective ways of reinforcing good behavior and avoiding situations which encourage unethical or non-objective behavior should be thoroughly discussed.

An underlying theme in the Project Star module is that learning what behavior is ethical and what is not is a process that begins early in life and continues through adulthood. The module recommends that officers should benefit from the experience of others; they should interview teachers, ministers, parents and case workers to determine what issues of right and wrong occur often among the people with whom they deal, and how those issues are eventually reconciled.

Project Star's sophisticated approach to increasing the ethical awareness of police recruits seems sound. It avoids to a great degree the lecture approach and "sermonizing" about the subject of police ethics. As with other innovative approaches, however, the question of the effectiveness of Project Star has yet to be resolved. Can ethics be taught to young adults, or is ethical conduct totally the result of early ethical conditioning through the family, school, or religious affiliation? That question was left unresolved for the Anti-Corruption Management Project. The staff of the Project generally felt that ethical conditioning can be useful and effective. Combined with the continuity of strong moral leadership from command level personnel, ethical conditioning may eventually change a corrupt department into a highly ethical one.

VIII
Guidelines for the Administrator in Developing and Implementing an Anti-Corruption Program

The Project staff felt that a step-by-step summary of the essential factors involved in defining, locating, and measuring corruption; policy and program development; and program implementation would be useful to police administrators. What follows, therefore, is an outline of essential ingredients of this manual, without the narrative text. The outline is designed as a worksheet for the administrator to aid him in logically pursuing the development and implementation of an anti-corruption program.

DEFINE CORRUPTION

—Establish a working definition of police corruption.
  —What is corruption and what is not corruption in your city.

—What do political authorities consider as corrupt activities on the part of the police?

—What activities do the police consider corrupt?

　—Are gratuities like free meals, free uniform cleaning, etc., commonplace and accepted?

　—Do all or some police officers accept such gratuities?

—What police activities do the public consider corrupt?

　—Does the public accept and encourage petty gratuities? Or does the public complain?

　—Does the acceptance of gratuities result in preferred treatment or non-supervision of those who "give?"

—What are your own conceptions of corruption?

　—Can you live with the definition developed?

—If familiar with the department, the answers to these questions will be apparent.

　—If unfamiliar, it may be necessary to develop some way to measure attitudes or perhaps to conduct interviews with those individuals (police, government officials, academics, media, etc.) who may have the answers.

DETERMINE THE NATURE OF CORRUPTION

—Begin with your definition of police corruption.

　—Approach the problem within the framework you have developed.

—While you must take a positive anti-corruption stance, do not initiate an anti-corruption program immediately after appointment or, in the case of an incumbent chief, immediately after deciding to develop and implement a formal anti-corruption program.

　—You must assess the problem before developing remedies.

　—If authorities press for immediate action, caution them on the dangers of premature, unplanned strategies.

—If necessary, meet with the prosecuting authorities to gain insight into the problem and its extent.

　—Indicate your total commitment to reforming the department and your willingness to assist authorities in every way.

　—If newly appointed, obtain as complete and detailed a

portrait as possible of suspected officers, ineffective and non-supportive commanders, supportive commanders.
—If problem is extensive, institute regular schedule of meetings with the prosecutor to obtain updates on current investigations.
—Meet individually with top staff of department on corruption problem.
  —Obtain their individual assessment of nature and extent of corruption problem.
    —Determine if their assessment is realistic.
    —Do they have strong positive attitudes toward integrity?
  —Obtain their assessment of overall attitudes of police officers toward police corruption.
  —Solicit their ideas on how to deal with the problem.
    —Identify those who are not supportive of taking strong action against wrongdoers.
  —Determine if top staff has complete confidence in the leadership and performance of the internal affairs unit.
    —If they have doubts, identify the reasons for those doubts.
    —What suggestions do they have for enhancing the performance of the internal affairs unit?
  —Are staff members supportive of the work of the prosecutor in addressing police corruption?
    —Have they given the prosecutor complete cooperation?
  —Determine what affirmative action top staff members have taken to address corruption problems in their own commands or units.
  —If any of the top staff are involved in current investigations, ask them, without infringing on their rights, for an explanation of their conduct.
—Obtain complete briefing on all corruption problems within the department from the internal affairs unit.
  —Discuss past performance of internal affairs.
    —Use information revealed in your interviews with prosecutor, and top department staff.
  —Determine what is the major focus of internal affairs.
    —How are complaints generated?
    —Does the unit engage in self-initiated investigations?

—Does the unit conduct any type of integrity-testing?

—Obtain corruption assessment of individual commands and commanders.

—Obtain assessment of overall attitudes of police officers towards police corruption.

—If applicable, meet with news and media people who "exposed" particular problems.

—Establish an immediate rapport and line of communication with the media.

—Meet informally with small groups of police officers and mid-level supervisors.

—Direct discussions to the subject of police corruption.

—Solicit suggestions and recommendations for improvement.

—Display a positive attitude at all times.

At this point, you should have a fairly accurate picture of the nature and scope of the problems of corruption within the department. It is entirely possible that the "problem" may be found to be minimal or even non-existent, because the corrupt police officers involved may all have been identified and suspended or fired. If so, there may be no need to change policy or implement new programs.

OBTAINING COMMITMENTS FROM AUTHORITIES

—With information on the nature and scope of the police corruption problem, meet with the mayor, Board of Commissioners, Town Council, or other appropriate municipal representatives and inform them of your intention to take action to remedy the problem.

—Brief the authorities on the state of corruption in the department.

—Emphasize the need for change.

—Determine the position of the political authorities on enforcement of those corruption-prone laws that regulate gambling, vice, narcotics, and Sunday business hours.

—Obtain a strong commitment for support of your policy on corruption and your anti-corruption program.

—Obtain commitment to freely address the problems.
—Ensure that there will be no political involvement in policy or programs developed. For a newly appointed or "reform" chief, a similar meeting will presumably have occurred prior to appointment.

DEVELOPMENT OF AN ANTI-CORRUPTION POLICY

—Your policy will depend on the nature of the problems to be addressed as identified by you after consulting with local officials and subordinates within your department.
  —Broad policy statements as well as statements that deal with specific and prevalent forms of corrupt behavior should be forceful and clear.
    —Attempts to be all inclusive and address every possible form of corruption can slow serious efforts to develop policy and cause cynical attitudes among officers.
    —All serious forms of corruption should be clear and specific with detailed instructions to subordinate superiors for handling observed violations.
—Consider ways to impart your policy.
  —State your overall policy on police corruption personally to as many officers as possible.
    —Consider an address to all ranking officers.
    —Keep your remarks brief.
    —Emphasize that the development of police integrity and the elimination of police corruption is the personal responsibility of each and every commander and supervisor.
      —Indicate most emphatically that commanders and supervisors will be held strictly accountable for police corruption in their command.
    —The tone of the remarks should be positive.
      —By developing a corruption-free department, the department stands in a stronger position for demanding salary increases.
      —Emphasize the rewards of a positive self-image, personal pride, and professionalism.
    —Solicit the assistance of your subordinates in addressing the problem.

—Ask for suggestions in developing your program.

—Put each commander and supervisor on notice that he will be responsible for developing an anti-corruption program in his own command, unit, or precinct.

 —Make it clear that anti-corruption activities will no longer be confined to the internal affairs unit.

—Direct each commander and supervisor to convey your message to the members of his command.

—Ask for the resignation of all those who feel they cannot support your policy.

—If not already in existence, publish and distribute to every member of the department a code of ethics.

 —If the department presently has a code, review it and rewrite it if necessary.

 —Several versions of a police code of ethics are used throughout the nation. If necessary, borrow from them and adopt a code to fit your department's needs.

 —Attempt to direct the code to the specific corruption areas that have caused problems in your department.

 —Publish a short order with the code that in essence demands the strictest adherence to its provisions.

—Review all existing orders, procedures, manuals on police corruption for relevancy and updating.

 —If non-existent or obsolete, rewrite the department procedures or policies on prohibited activities.

  —prohibited activities should be specific enough to include all forms of existing or suspected corruption within the department.

  —The list of prohibited activities must be made available to each member of the department. A chapter or section in the department manual or rules specifically indicating proscribed activities would serve the purpose.

—Publish and distribute specific replies to legitimate inquiries on possible corrupt activities.

 —You can expect requests for clarification on department policy regarding prohibited conduct, particularly those involving off-duty activities, acceptance of rewards, etc. Therefore, strongly consider publishing on a regular basis, the department policy on each of these issues.

—These replies must be realistic, positive, and offer thorough explanations.

—Directly solicit from individual members requests for clarification of policy on corruption.

—Have requests directed to a police board of ethics or another similar committee like the board of commissioners, local chiefs association, etc.

—Ensure that your policy is communicated to all members and thoroughly understood by them.

—If necessary, appear at infrequent and unannounced times before outgoing platoons and repeat your message in a positive manner.

—Ask various personnel officers and supervisors for feedback on the reception of policies.

—Utilize departmental house organ, newsletter, or memoranda to stop rumors and clarify possible inconsistencies.

DESIGNING THE ANTI-CORRUPTION PROGRAM

—Form a committee, representing all ranks in the department, to plan and design an ethical standards program.

—Organize the committee into groups to work on different aspects of the program like policy implementation, training, and evaluation.

—Give the committee a reasonable deadline for presenting a completed design and program.

—Maximum time allowed should not exceed six months.

—Provide for periodic updates on the committee's progress or lack of progress.

—Appoint as chairman of the committee, a ranking officer who has the confidence and support of the department's rank and file.

—Ensure that the committee utilizes focused agendas which make the group work on specific issues.

—Your policies, which have already been announced, will provide the committee with a framework for action.

—Emphasis should be placed on the preventive nature of the plan.

—Except in rare cases, the plan should not be retroactive.

—Provide for extensive review of the plan prior to implementation.

—The plan should be reviewed by top staff, unit heads, and supervisors.

—It is critical that a representative group of first line personnel also be permitted to review the plan.

—Consideration should be given to any comments made by the reviewers.

—A final review of the plan by the department's legal staff will be necessary prior to implementation.

—Present a final plan which includes:

—specific provisions.

—delineation and purpose of new policies and the methods of carrying out these policies.

—possible sanctions for violation.

—organizational changes, if necessary.

—role of training and education.

—a statement of the goal to be achieved.

—who is responsible for carrying out each aspect of the plan.

—Select one commander to be responsible for administering the program.

—Don't attempt to be the enforcer yourself unless you head a small department.

—Select an individual in whom you have complete trust.

—He must be willing to accept the "flak" that will be directed at him.

—Since the program will be innovative, a new face might help to obtain vital support.

—Inform the political authorities of the elements of your plan.

—Emphasize the need for total governmental support of the plan.

—Advise the mayor or head of local government that pressure may be forthcoming from various business interests like licensed premises or contractors which may be adversely affected by the plan.

—Stress the need for total commitment and enforcement once the plan is implemented.

—If compromises are to be made, they must come *prior* to implementation.
—Consider how the plan will be released to the media.
  —Copies of the plan can be released to the media at a press conference.
    —Describe the purpose of the plan.
    —Emphasize its positive nature.
  —Do not attempt to avoid the press, evade questions, or conceal the plan.

IMPLEMENTING THE PLAN

—Implement the plan on a specific date to take effect immediately.
—If necessary, meet with union representatives or groups of police officers.
  —Explain the positive nature of the plan and its goal of promoting a professional image.
  —If unions and police officers were well represented on the planning committee, your task should not be difficult.
—Remember that the key to successful implementation is acceptance of the program by first line officers and supervisors.
  —The provisions of the new program must be clearly stated and *enforced.*
  —Enforcement must be uniform.
    —Ensure that commanders act uniformly and consistently in exacting punishment.
—Don't be alarmed if you encounter a morale problem at the outset.
  —Clear statements of policy, uniform action, and full support of the actions of commanders will overcome morale problems.
—Provide for continuous feedback on progress.
  —Build an evaluation component into the plan to determine its effectiveness.
    —Include specific objectives and milestones.
    —Use measuring devices like record reviews, civilian complaints, or bribery arrests.

—Continously indicate your support of the program.

—Keep the rank and file informed of the progress being made.

—Take swift action against commanders and supervisors who fail to support the plan.

—Ensure that violators are identified and punished.

TRAINING

—Institute a training program in ethical standards.

—If a training program already exists, review it carefully for relevancy and content.

—Consider adopting the "ethical awareness" format.

—Have research done to develop material relevant to your situation.

—Make the program as ethical as possible.

—Focus on three kinds of training:

—Recruit Training.

—Keep the training realistic and geared toward actual street situations.

—Use the role-playing approach for effectiveness.

—Consider the F.B.I. agent training program in ethical standards as a model.

—The length of the course will depend on the extent of your problem.

—In your recruit course, consider instruction in the following subject areas:

—departmental policies and procedures and ethical standards.

—historical and social aspects of police corruption.

—the psychological costs of police corruption.

—practical exercises.

—In-Service Training.

—For experienced officers, use a different approach like small-group seminars.

—Become personally involved in in-service training.

—A dialogue with the chief will clarify misunderstandings about departmental policy.

—Select instructors who are street-oriented.

—Avoid using police academy or internal affairs personnel as instructors.

—Street supervisors will relate more easily and be more acceptable to experienced officers.

—Consider instruction in the following subject areas:
   —ethics.
   —the investigation of misconduct and the role of the internal affairs unit.
   —practical exercises.

—Supervisory and Management Training.
   —You must put heavy emphasis on the training of supervisors and managers because the key to an effective anti-corruption program lies with supervisors and management personnel.
   —Appear personally at each training session to address the class.
      —Specify what is expected from each commander and supervisor.

—Consider instruction in the following areas:
   —Problems in ethical standards.
   —The supervisor's role in combatting misconduct and possible corrupt activities.

Appendix
Briefing
of the
Chief-Designate

As a result of interviewing dozens of commissioners and chiefs of police, the Project staff believes that a new chief of police should have the opportunity to be briefed by other chiefs before taking office. Data gathered in the Anti-Corruption Management Project's national survey of internal affairs indicates that 15 of the 104 chiefs who responded had less than one year in office, and 47 had less than three years. According to a recent handbook, (Kelly, 1975) the processing of a new chief after he has been selected is as important as the selection process itself. The authors of the handbook recommend a training period during which "a chief-designate can travel, visit other departments" to develop his problem-solving techniques through the mutual exchange of ideas with other chiefs. This orientation period is particularly important for a "reform chief." The value of briefing a chief-designate in anti-corruption administration is illustrated in the interview that follows.

The interview was conducted during an in-depth study of a law enforcement agency that had recently been the subject of a major scandal. The scandal involved collusion among the police and local politicians to extort protection money from local businessmen. As a result several political figures, the chief of police and several of his subordinates were indicted and subsequently convicted.

Subsequently, a new reform chief from outside the jurisdiction was appointed. The interview was conducted approximately eight months after the new chief*had taken office, and he recreates the situation prior to his administration and the steps he took to reorganize and redirect the agency. The interview is useful, because it describes the kinds of experience any new chief of police may expect as he takes office after a serious corruption scandal. It also illustrates the kind of processing program that should be furnished to a chief after he has been selected.

The chief's name and jurisdiction are confidential. However, the jurisdiction concerned is a county, and the chief's agency employs approximately 150 sworn officers to patrol the area's 127 square miles. The chief had been a chief in a department about one half the size of his new one, and he has a reputation for progressive and innovative leadership.

SELECTING A NEW CHIEF

QUESTION: Can you explain how you first became aware that a national search for a police chief in County X was being conducted?
ANSWER: I received a letter from the County Manager, indicating that my name had been given to him as one of several professionals around the country who might be interested in the position of Chief. He indicated that the previous chief had been indicted on charges of extortion and police corruption.
QUESTION: Do you know who gave the County Manager your name?
ANSWER: I suspect my name may have come from the International Association of Chiefs of Police or the Police Foundation. Both of these agencies were aware that I was interested in being interviewed.

QUESTION: How did they become aware of your interest?

ANSWER: Through personal and constant contacts with me over the years and knowledge that I was looking for a position of greater responsibility.

QUESTION: You were told of various types of corruption in this department. How did you personally learn the degree to which officers were involved?

ANSWER: Through conducting an intensive investigation of my own in this area. I knew that in terms of my initial discussions, the Manager and County Council were conducting a background investigation on me, which I felt was only right and proper. I also visited them. I was doing my own investigation to determine to my satisfaction that the county really wanted a change and that the corruption problem could be dealt with effectively.

QUESTION: What did you do? What was your approach?

ANSWER: I contacted people in a broad spectrum of governmental service and community services.

QUESTION: How did you select the people you wanted to interview?

ANSWER: I contacted people in federal, state, and local government. I contacted people of various faiths and denominations. I contacted persons in some of the larger industries through contacts I had.

QUESTION: Did you contact them by telephone?

ANSWER: By telephone, yes.

QUESTION: And how did you introduce yourself on the telephone?

ANSWER: It was relatively easy, because of the fact that I was under final consideration was well publicized in County X. There was really no difficulty in telling people who I was and why I was calling. I explained to them that I was specifically interested in knowing what their reaction was to the idea of corruption being eliminated in the county.

QUESTION: Was there any one factor that convinced you that they indeed wanted reform and would give you a completely free hand in straightening out the department?

ANSWER: I'd say there were two factors. I was very favorably impressed with the County Manager as someone who wanted change and who would be totally supportive. There was also unanimous commitment by the County Council and by people in the community who contacted me that a change was desirable and was wanted by everyone. It was clear to me that they would support an anti-corruption endeavor fully and without qualifications.

In an open meeting with the County Council, prior to making my decision to come here, they asked me some very pointed questions for about an hour. When they were through I asked them two of my own. I said, "First, I want to know, right here and now, and in front of all these reporters, what is your position on the enforcement of vice laws? Should they be strictly enforced?" They unanimously agreed, without qualification, that the laws should be strictly enforced. They told me that they would totally support a strict program. The second question I asked was, "Would the Council support total reorganization of the police department, providing that the reorganization would be in accordance with established administrative practice?" They unanimously agreed.

QUESTION: It has been said that at various stages of reforming a police department, the chief has to show different leadership styles. How would you describe your style for the first six to eight months, and do you have any ideas about changing your present style?

ANSWER: I think probably — I don't want to use the term, "relax," because it may give the wrong impression — but I think I will be able to afford to change my leadership style as we progress further and everyone becomes firmly convinced that I will not tolerate any kind of transgression or any unprofessionalism. At the present time, I tend to be extremely autocratic as opposed to my style in my former department, because I find it necessary. However, I don't want to appear unreceptive to the ideas of other people, and I try all the time to staff people at all levels. I also meet with the patrolmen approximately once a month to discuss their gripes and to allow them to present viewpoints or exchange ideas. I'm a great believer in participative management, but because of the nature of an anti-corruption drive, I find it necessary to be more autocratic than I usually might be.

QUESTION: Was the former chief of this department indicted?

ANSWER: Yes.

QUESTION: Was an acting chief appointed when the former chief was indicted?

ANSWER: Yes.

QUESTION: Is the acting chief still in the department?

ANSWER: Yes, he is. He's currently a captain in charge of the uniform division.

QUESTION: Was there any feeling on the part of anybody here that somebody local was going to head the department, or was it a foregone conclusion that the County Manager would look outside the state for a new chief?

ANSWER: It was a foregone conclusion based on a prior report. The acting chief had also stated at the time of the indictment that he was not interested in being chief. Given the tradition and tarnished image of the department, he felt he could not accomplish reform at this time. However, he was one officer in the department whose integrity was above question. As a result, he had been placed in a position of limited responsibility and had had no direct say in the operation of the department.

QUESTION: Before you became chief, did you feel that you needed some kind of confidante whom you could trust?

ANSWER: That's basically it. I hired an administrative assistant whom I refer to as Assistant to the Chief, to help me with many various tasks. His position has evolved, and he is now in charge of the Office of Inspectional Services. I needed someone whom I trusted implicitly and with whom I could discuss anything at any time.

QUESTION: Would you recommend that a reform chief have a trusted assistant?

ANSWER: Absolutely, absolutely. In a department of this size, a trusted assistant is absolutely necessary. In a larger department probably, more than one assistant is needed. In fact, I had suggested that at least two people be hired here to assist me.

QUESTION: Were there any personal threats to you concerning your taking over the department and making it known that you were going to clean up the county?

ANSWER: After a period of time, during which we made some very definite progress in suppressing vice, we became aware of very definite threats of bodily harm against me and against an attorney who was representing the public service district, police and fire departments. The fire department, serving the area in which alleged vice activity was occurring, was involved in a joint operation of vice inspections with the police. Because of the emphasis on vice activities, these inspections were frequent and thorough. The investigations tended to indicate that perhaps these threats were low-level. Our response was to immediately investigate persons who were making threats and to fully publicize the matter of the threats themselves. We identified some individuals who may have made the threats, but they denied making them. We learned subsequently that threats had subsided but that other alternative approaches would be used to fight our attempts to suppress vice.

QUESTION: Namely what?

ANSWER: Through the use of all available money, legal expertise, and whenever possible, legal manipulation.

ANATOMY OF POLICE CORRUPTION

QUESTION: Could you give us a little history about County X before you arrived? What led to the former police chief's indictment and how did it become known that the department was corrupt?

ANSWER: The chief's indictment was the result of a federal indictment based upon allegations by fourteen bar owners who had claimed that they were paying police for protection or police were extorting payments from them.

QUESTION: Did they ever complain to the City Manager, or did they go directly to the federal authorities?

ANSWER: They went directly to the federal authorities. You have to remember that prior to the indictment of the chief of police, the chairman of the county council and another councilman were indicted on charges of extortion or corruption in connection with the same bar owners.

QUESTION: Apparently corruption existed not only in the police department but in county government for a considerable period before the scandal broke. In terms of these bar owners and in terms of all collusion between the police and the city government, do you have any kind of feeling or evidence that an organized group of people were involved in these activities?

ANSWER: There's no question in my mind that there was an organized group. There is reputed to be a group in County X which would not be classified as organized crime in the traditional sense, but very definitely would be similar to organized crime. The group dealt with various and diversified criminal activities conducted over a long period of time on local, statewide and inter-state levels. I'm certain that we can very justifiably call this organized, syndicated crime as it exists elsewhere in the United States.

QUESTION: These individuals controlling the county certainly weren't going to allow one individual, a new chief of police, to destroy their comfortable operation. What was their response when they learned that you were going to be the new police chief and that you intended to reform the department?

ANSWER: After the initial physical threats which never materialized, we heard rumors that they were going to take a "wait and see" attitude or that they were going to move their operations elsewhere.

QUESTION: How, specifically, were the police involved with organized crime?

ANSWER: The police were allegedly involved in protection through the direction and control of the chairman of the county council. The chief of police was alleged to have done two things. First, he precluded, by delegating the responsibility to the vice squad, the possibility of uniformed officers checking any licensed or unlicensed premises, where vice activities might be taking place. Second, he is alleged to have exercised such control over the vice squad that any premises that paid the squad would be protected against raids or inspection checks and in effect would be left alone.

QUESTION: Were these the actual charges on which the chief was indicted?

ANSWER: That's right.

QUESTION: Although these particular bar owners who brought the suit were being harrassed by the police, why would they go to the federal government to say that they didn't want to pay local police for protection? What were the threats made against these establishments if they did not pay for protection?

ANSWER: Strict enforcement would take place, and arrests would be made.

QUESTION: For what? For engaging in vice, supposedly?

ANSWER: Very definitely.

QUESTION: And the bar owners still went to the federal government?

ANSWER: That's correct. Some were subpoenaed to testify before a federal grand jury, and as outlined in the federal indictments, they testified that money pay-offs and carnal bribes were made.

QUESTION: There apparently seems to be a point of diminishing returns regarding whether or not a vice operation can continue in business. Apparently they were reaching the point where the returns were not justifying their activities.

ANSWER: That's correct. According to the federal indictment, the charges involved gambling, prostitution, and violations of the regulations governing establishments where alcoholic beverages are dispensed.

QUESTION: Again, why would fourteen bar owners engaging in illegal operations go to federal authorities and say that they did not want to pay local police for protection?

ANSWER: In essence, the bar owners alleged charges of racketeering activities by the chief of police and other officers. Those activities included solicitation and acceptance of bribes.

QUESTION: But why did the bar-owners bypass the state?

ANSWER: Perhaps they lacked confidence in state officials. They felt they wanted something done about a situation which they felt was deplorable.

QUESTION: How many officers were involved?

ANSWER: A few.

QUESTION: The federal agency was the F.B.I.?

ANSWER: Yes.

QUESTION: And what did they do?

ANSWER: The F.B.I. conducted an intensive, highly complex investigation using information from the bar owners, police officers, and other sources.

QUESTION: Did they interview policemen?

ANSWER: They interviewed some police officers, yes.

QUESTION: Did the police know they were being interviewed by the F.B.I.?

ANSWER: They did.

QUESTION: And what kind of effect did the F.B.I. interviews have? Did the police chief learn about them?

ANSWER: I'm not sure. I feel certain that he was aware through conversations with officers that an investigation was underway prior to his indictment.

QUESTION: How many officers have worked on the vice squad?

ANSWER: From two to six men, depending upon the degree of suppression that was being attempted.

QUESTION: Do you think that most of the force knew what was occurring with the vice squad?

ANSWER: I think most of the officers on the force knew but felt unable to do anything about it.

QUESTION: That vice squad was comprised of a sergeant and three to six policemen?

ANSWER: It varied during the last five years. At times there were a corporal and a detective, or a sergeant and a detective, or a sergeant and a corporal, plus three or four officers. One sergeant was transferred back and forth to the vice squad during the last six months of my predecessor's administration. Whenever they wanted some additional enforcement emphasized they'd transfer him to the vice squad. When they wanted to kind of ease up, they'd transfer him back into uniform.

QUESTION: Didn't he realize what they were doing?

ANSWER: He did.

QUESTION: And he never said anything?

ANSWER: I'm certain he was aware that he was being used.

QUESTION: What about narcotics? Dealers probably would not report that they were being asked to pay police for protection. I'm just wondering if the police were involved with narcotics.

ANSWER: There were allegations, but they were not supported by any real evidence.

QUESTION: As far as you can determine, would it be appro-

priate to describe the sergeant who was in charge of the vice
squad as being a "bag-man"?

ANSWER: He is alleged to have been at that time.

QUESTION: The sergeant's assignment to the vice squad was
rather permanent while the other members of the squad were
transferred on a regular basis?

ANSWER: Correct. The sergeant had a relatively permanent
assignment, usually for three or four years.

QUESTION: What other sections of the department were
corrupt?

ANSWER: A real lack of confidence existed in the officers
assigned to narcotics investigation, but there was no hard evidence of any kind to substantiate that they were in any way
corrupt. They were, however, felt to be very definitely ineffective by every other law enforcement agency I contacted
and by people in the community. They were not trusted by
informants, by other agencies, or by many of the men within
the department. Other officers wouldn't come to them with
information and wouldn't supply them with leads.

QUESTION: What would happen if they were supplied with
leads?

ANSWER: The cases for some reason or another would never
result in successful conclusions.

QUESTION: Did anything unfortunate ever happen to the informants?

ANSWER: Several informants claimed that their covers had
been blown, and consequently their sources of information
were eliminated. That informants were no longer available to
police might indicate that members of the narcotics squad
were communicating members of organized crime. There was
also a lack of supervisory initiative, and police were not provided with any real guidelines or goals and objectives. In addition, the morale factor was crucial, because the officers were
either aware of what was taking place or they had a lot of
suspicions. The turn-over rate which was relatively high also
caused problems.

QUESTION: Did you ever hear that your predecessor would
use his power to influence an officer?

ANSWER: He was alleged to have used his authority arbi-
trarily and capriciously.

QUESTION: What about other kinds of violations? Would he ever tell an officer that maybe it would be a good idea to check out a certain situation or to tell him to forget about another kind of situation?

ANSWER: I've heard of examples.

QUESTION: Involving what kinds of policing?

ANSWER: Vice narcotics, and particular individuals who might have been involved in the underworld in the community.

QUESTION: He would say, "Lay off"?

ANSWER: Maybe not specifically that, but he might indicate that perhaps their efforts might be better directed in another area.

QUESTION: Let's say the officer operated in an area which the chief had said was off-limits. If the officer continued to work in that area, was he punished in any way?

ANSWER: Yes.

QUESTION: What method did the chief use to enforce his suggestion?

ANSWER: It was alleged that the retribution was usually a transfer to an undesirable area far from the officer's home or removal from the detective bureau.

QUESTION: Did other supervisors ever offer similar suggestions?

ANSWER: That's alleged of a few.

QUESTION: Are they still employed but unindicted?

ANSWER: Some are, yes. Since I took office, these practices have stopped.

QUESTION: Was it fairly well known that as a vice-officer one could make money?

ANSWER: I think it was fairly common knowledge that if you managed to get an assignment to the vice squad, that you'd do well.

QUESTION: What do you mean, "do well"?

ANSWER: In terms of carnal or monetary bribes.

QUESTION: When you're talking about money, what amounts of it are you suggesting?

ANSWER: Amounts varied with the officers involved. In some cases, it's alleged to have been hundreds of dollars, and in other cases it's alleged to be thousands of dollars.

QUESTION: Hundreds a week? Hundreds a month?

ANSWER: Hundreds a week.

QUESTION: And thousands a week?

ANSWER: Thousands a week for specific things.

QUESTION: What would be worth a thousand a week?

ANSWER: In one situation it's alleged that a pay-off of that amount would be for not challenging a license application to the state.

QUESTION: How many people would get a thousand a week?

ANSWER: Very few.

QUESTION: How many would get approximately a hundred a week or get sexual services?

ANSWER: Probably several police. Those kinds of pay-offs are alleged against three intermediary officers who are under indictment now.

QUESTION: Just considering those who were provided with women, how many of the hundred and fifty people in the department participated?

ANSWER: At least once?

QUESTION: Yes.

ANSWER: I would guess about twenty-five.

QUESTION: If twenty-five people were feloniously corrupt, consequently, a sizeable portion of the department was not. The Knapp Commission described the most seriously corrupt as "meateaters" and the less serious violators as "grass-eaters". Was it a policy within the department that one-sixth of the force would be allowed to be corrupt within police ranks?

ANSWER: It was commonly accepted that gratuities would be available. In other words, police could get free meals, discounts, theater tickets, and tickets of admission to circuses.

QUESTION: These things existed for just about a hundred percent of the patrolmen at that time?

ANSWER: Maybe not to all, but certainly for the majority.

QUESTION: But at least twenty-five people were accepting considerably more than that?

ANSWER: I would say so.

QUESTION: Do you have any feeling at all about whether

or not taking petty graft — obviously a number of police officers were not engaged in petty graft because they went to the Federal Bureau of Investigation — had any effect on the men reporting more serious violations of trust?

ANSWER: I think so.

QUESTION: Petty graft was not defined by them as corruption, was it?

ANSWER: No one told them not to engage in petty graft. I'm a great believer in what is called the bilker of corruption. On one end of the spectrum, you have people who will always take, and they're a small minority, maybe five percent. On the other end you've got people who will never take, again five percent. Between these two groups, you've got the majority in the bilker category who are waiting to be told, "Yes, it's all right to take gratuities," or "No, it's not all right to accept gratuities."

QUESTION: And in the absence of policy they go ahead and make their own policy.

ANSWER: Right. Exactly.

QUESTION: And their policy says in effect that all kinds of petty graft is acceptable.

ANSWER: Right.

QUESTION: How long will it take the men to generate their own resistance to corruption?

ANSWER: Now I think they would generate resistance very effectively. Using long range, positive efforts built on very strong foundations, it would probably be two to three years.

DEVELOPING ANTI- CORRUPTION POLICIES

QUESTION: What were some of the first administrative moves you made to reform the department?

ANSWER: The first changes were in the vice squad and the uniformed division. The second day I was in office, I assigned joint responsibility to the uniform patrol division and the vice squad to check licensed premises for indications of vice law violations. The uniform officers had not been accustomed to checking these premises. They didn't know what to look for, and they were unsure of themselves in terms of making an appropriate charge when they saw a violation. Members of the vice squad had to intensively train patrol officers for about a week.

QUESTION: Did you disband the old vice squad?

ANSWER: No, the squad had been partially disbanded before my arrival by the acting chief.

QUESTION: Could you describe your first meeting with members of the department?

ANSWER: They wanted to know, first of all, if I had a broom. They wanted to know how big it was, how wide it was, and how I would sweep with it. I told them that I wanted good law enforcement. I told them specifically that they were not to be afraid to enforce the law, and that I would back them a hundred percent. We were going to professionalize; we were going to improve their image, but I was going to need their support.

QUESTION: Did they believe you?

ANSWER: Their reaction was enthusiastic.

QUESTION: What about those unindicted people who might have been involved in corruption but who were still members of the department? How did they react to your remarks?

ANSWER: At least on the surface they reacted favorably. To my way of thinking, they paid lip service to change. Several remained under internal investigation, however, because the investigation process was severely hampered by a lack of available information.

QUESTION: Did you give any kind of general amnesty to anyone previously involved in corrupt policy?

ANSWER: Obviously not.

QUESTION: Did you have evidence on some people who had been contaminated during the previous administration? Could you forget that evidence as long as those officers adhered to your policies?

ANSWER: Again, each case is different, and my reaction depends upon the wrongdoing in which an officer was involved. Was it major involvement, or was it minor; what were the circumstances under which they were involved and what was the extent of their involvement? I did try to insulate the department from them as much as possible by placing them in non-sensitive positions.

QUESTION: Let us assume that corruption is a kind of by-product of the system. Suppose an individual totally reforms in your opinion and totally accepts your way of operating. Can you just forget what he was in the past?

ANSWER: That depends, but I can't forget an indictable felony or misdemeanor.

QUESTION: You have issued a general order which indicates policy regarding integrity and professional standards. How is the general order enforced, and what kind of sanctions are there for violating rules? Secondly, how do you learn whether someone is breaking those rules?

ANSWER: If someone breaks rules, he or she is brought up on disciplinary charges, depending on the gravity of violation.

QUESTION: If someone take a free cup of coffee and you learn about it, what do you do?

ANSWER: The person probably gets an oral reprimand from his supervisor. The matter would come to my attention in the following way: a civilian might phone the department and say, "Hey, we saw three of your officers drinking coffee at a restaurant. And they left and didn't even pay. They didn't even leave a tip. I think that's deplorable. Now what are you going to do about it?" Well, I would phone the captain and suggest that he talk to the lieutenant, and suggest that the lieutenant talk to the sergeant and that the sergeant talk to the men.

QUESTION: Is there a book that lists disciplinary actions?

ANSWER: Yes, there is a general order dealing with discipline. Punishments can include oral reprimands, fines, or suspensions.

QUESTION: Did you ever give a fine?

ANSWER: No, I have not given a fine as yet. I have asked for resignations.

QUESTION: For what kind of activity?

ANSWER: For testimony before a federal grand jury under immunity that an officer accepted carnal bribes in connection with vice enforcement activity.

QUESTION: Did the officer resign?

ANSWER: He did.

QUESTION: Is there anything in writing that says you can

force a man to resign?

ANSWER: No, but there are written procedures that permit me to fire him.

QUESTION: Even though he was granted immunity?

ANSWER: Yes, because those are two separate things, immunity from criminal prosecution and the right to keep a job.

QUESTION: When you came to County X, you were obviously changing some long established relationships between the police and the community. You stopped police from accepting discounted meals, free cups of coffee, and free entry into the movies. Did you work with the press or with the public to make the changes known?

ANSWER: I definitely worked with the press.

QUESTION: What did you do?

ANSWER: As each anti-corruption measure was announced, we talked with the press at length about the necessity for the policy, what the policy represented, and what the effect of the policy would be.

QUESTION: Did you get mail from the public?

ANSWER: Yes.

QUESTION: What kind of mail?

ANSWER: Very favorable, indicating that reform has been a long time coming and that they supported it.

QUESTION: You also discovered certain locations within County X where officers went for free meals. Did you personally go to those places or write to the proprietors of the restaurants?

ANSWER: No, I found that that wasn't necessary. However, I would have resorted to that kind of an approach, if necessary. One place in particular had hung a plaque prominently in the lobby. It had been presented by community police to the restaurant, citing the place for their cooperation over the past years. The plaque publicly thanks the restaurant for its cooperation. Using the chain of command approach, I asked a supervisor to visit the premises and to tell the owner that I did not approve of that plaque in the lobby, particularly in light of our policy. I didn't care if he hung the plaque in his office, but publicly, I did not want it on display. I also told the supervisor to inform the manager that I would personally come to see him, that the public display was not in conformity with our policy, and that I would place his establishment off limits to my officers. I didn't have to actually threaten the manager, but I would definitely have placed that restuarant or any other place off limits if a gratuity policy continued, or was found to be in effect.

QUESTION: What has been the response to your policy from other departments? Officers from three or four other jurisdictions are eating in the restaurants in your jurisdiction; they patrol similar areas. Other officers from other departments are allowed to accept free meals and other kinds of gratuities. The Project staff heard that as many as twenty bottles of liquor could be collected as Christmas presents by an officer. Do you get any feedback from other police chiefs or do the men get any feedback from other officers?

ANSWER: Yes, no doubt they do. The feedback from other chiefs has been positive, without exception.

QUESTION: Yet they haven't changed the policy in their departments?

ANSWER: In those other departments, particularly two city departments, I don't think they have had the corruption problem that we have had here in County X.

QUESTION: But isn't accepting gratuities corruption?

ANSWER: Sure, it is corruption, but I haven't discussed it with them at any length.

QUESTION: Do you feel that a newly appointed reformed chief has a tremendous advantage over a chief who wants to reform his department after being the chief for two or three years?

ANSWER: Definitely. And we try to reinforce our officers' attitudes. We have a copy of a letter that we use when Christmas presents are sent to us. We send the presents back with a letter which is tailor-made to meet the specific gift, be it a flower pot or a case of liquor.

QUESTION: Do the other departments react to receiving gifts in the same way?

ANSWER: I'm not sure. I've been so involved with my own department that I haven't had a chance to discuss gratuities with them. I'm certain that the other two chiefs do not approve of gratuities, and they're certainly against any forms of corruption.

QUESTION: There are so many situations similar to the acceptance of discounted meals, when your officers are side-by-side with other officers who pay different prices. What kind of reaction have you gotten from your officers?
ANSWER: I hear that they say, "Since you came here what have you given us? You've taken away our free meals, you've taken away our nice working hours, what have you given us?"
QUESTION: What do you say?
ANSWER: I've given them a police department that is as non-corrupt as I can make it.

Bibliography

Bahn, Charles. "The Psychosocial Costs of Police Corruption." New York: The John Jay Press, 1976.

Barker, Thomas and Julian B. Roebuck. *An Empirical Typology of Police Corruption: A Study in Organizational Deviance.* Springfield, Illinois: C.C. Thomas, 1974.

Beigel, Herbert. "The Closed Fraternity of Police and the Development of the Corrupt Attitude." New York: The John Jay Press, 1977.

Bracey, Dorothy Heid. "A Functional Approach to Police Corruption." New York: The John Jay Press, 1976.

Brown, William P. *The New York City Police Department Anti-Corruption Campaign: October 1970 — August 1972.* Unpublished. Albany, New York: State University of New York, 1972.

Burnham, David. "The Role of the Media in Controlling Corruption." New York: The John Jay Press, 1976.

California Commission on Peace Officer Standards and

Training. *Project Star: Role Performance and the Criminal Justice System, Volume I, II, and III.* Santa Cruz, California: Anderson-Davis Publishing Company, 1974.

Chin, Robert and Kenneth D. Benne. "General Strategies for Effecting Changes in Human Systems," in *The Planning of Change,* edited by Warren G. Bennis, Kenneth D. Benne, and Robert Chin. New York: Holt, Rinehart and Winston, 1969.

City of Los Angeles Police Department. *A Manual of the Los Angeles Police Department.* Los Angeles, California: Los Angeles Police Department, 1973.

City of New York Police Department. *General Guidelines of the Police Department Board of Ethics.* New York: Department of Police, 1973.

City of New York Police Department, *Integrity Control Anti-Corruption Manual.* New York, 1975.

Davis, Edward. *Canons of Police Ethics.* Los Angeles, California: Department of Police, 1974.

Duchaine, Nina. *The Literature of Police Corruption: Volume II: A Selected, Annotated Bibliography.* New York: The John Jay Press, 1979.

Fishman, Janet E. "Measuring Police Corruption." New York: The John Jay Press, 1978.

Goldstein, Herman. *Police Corruption: A Perspective on Its Nature and Control.* Washington, D.C.: Police Foundation, 1975.

Gorden, Raymond L. *Interviewing: Strategy, Techniques and Tactics,* Revised Edition. Homewood, Illinois: The Dorsey Press, 1975.

Hampton, David R., Charles E. Summer, and Ross A. Webber. *Organizational Behavior and the Practices of Management,* Revised Edition. Glenview, Illinois: Scott Foresman & Company, 1973.

Kelly, Michael J. *Police Chief Selection: A Handbook for Local Government.* Washington, D.C. Police Foundation and the International City Management Association, December, 1975.

Knapp Commission Report on Police Corruption, The. New York: George Braziller, 1973.

McCarthy, William, "A Police Administrator Looks at Police

Corruption." New York: The John Jay Press, 1976.

Meyer, John C. "Complaints of Police Corruption." New York: The John Jay Press, 1977.

Police Federation. *Supplement to the Police Federation Handbook of Police Discipline.* London: Police Federation, June, 1965.

National Advisory Commission on Criminal Justice Standards and Goals. *Police.* Washington, D.C.: U.S. Government Printing Office, 1973.

Shealy, Allan E. "The Role of Psychological Screening of Applicants," New York: The John Jay Press, 1976.

Sherman, Lawrence W. "City Politics, Police Administrators, and Corruption Control." New York: The John Jay Press, 1977.

Simpson, Antony E. *The Literature of Police Corruption: Volume I: A Guide to Bibliography and Theory.* New York: The John Jay Press, 1977.

Urban Institute. *Police Burglary Prevention Program.* Washington, D.C.: Urban Institute, 1975.

Ward, Richard H. *Manual for Robbery Control Projects.* New York: John Jay College of Criminal Justice, 1974.

Ware, Mitchell. "Developing a Police Anti-Corruption Capability," New York: The John Jay Press, 1977.

Wilson, James Q. *Varieties of Police Behavior.* Cambridge, Massachusetts, Harvard University Press, 1968.